WHITE RIVER, BROWN WATER

A record-making kayak journey down the Amazon

ALAN HOLMAN

HODDER AND STOUGHTON
LONDON SYDNEY AUCKLAND TORONTO

ACKNOWLEDGMENTS

I should like to thank David Cohen for his help in
approaching the publishing jungle, and my very patient
and tolerant editor, Margaret Body.

A.H.

British Library Cataloguing in Publication Data
Holman, Alan
  White river, brown water
  1. Kayaks—Amazon River   2. Amazon River—
  Description and travel
  I. Title
  918.1'1   F2546

  ISBN 0 340 34745 7

To my son
Steven

CONTENTS

ILLUSTRATIONS

between pages 96 and 97

* Reproduced by permission of the Susan Griggs Agency Ltd. All other photographs by the author.

WHITE RIVER, BROWN WATER

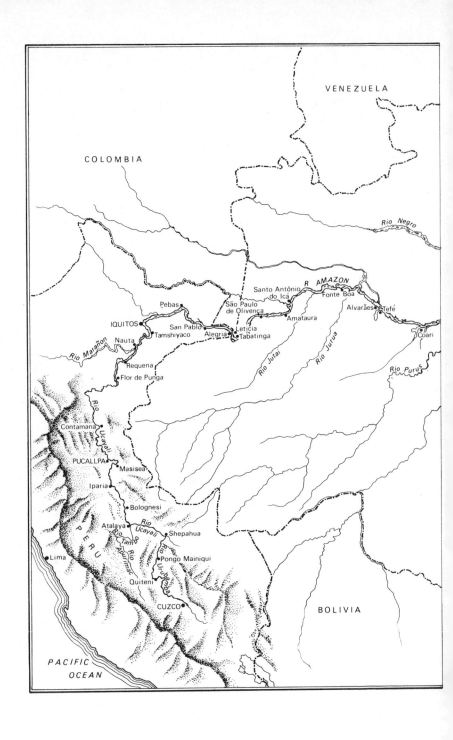

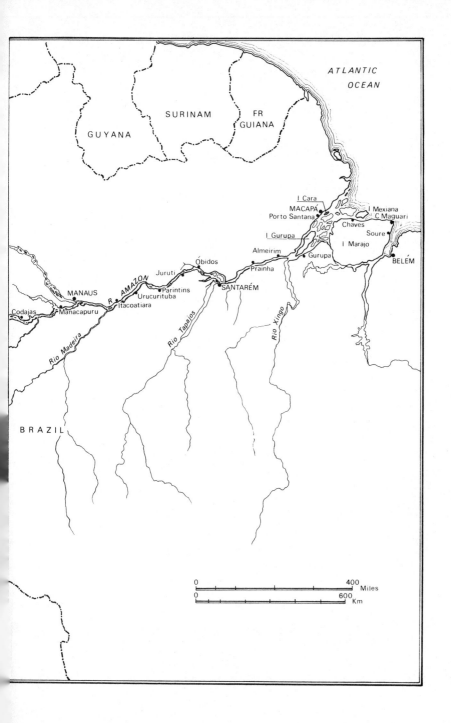

1   THE IDEA FORMS

The Amazon has always fascinated me: I have long felt its
secrecy, its size and its elusiveness to be a challenge. People are
constantly being swallowed up in its unexplored vastness; a
place of great mystery, I've always wondered what life there
was really like. I have also always wanted to create a world
record so I decided to combine these two desires; I would
canoe alone down the greatest river in the world, further than
any man had ever gone before.

The idea of making the canoe trip occurred to me when I was
in the Amazon area on unpaid leave from the Royal Australian
Air Force, pursuing my historical and geographical interests. I
had two more years to serve and then I would be free.
Meanwhile I would try to gather all the information I could
which would eventually help me on my solo expedition.

For two weeks in 1979, I travelled 2000 miles of the Amazon
in small cargo vessels, from Leticia to Belém, taking notes on
everything I saw, especially water conditions, possible
hazards, and potential supply points. I started to sketch the
ideal boat for the trip and make lists of all the cargo I would
need. The canoe would have to be large enough for all my
supplies and yet versatile enough to handle everything from
the white water of the Andes to the ocean conditions at the
mouth where the river was over 125 miles wide.

Maps! I would have to have maps but where could I get such
things? I asked the skippers of the vessels I travelled on but they
seemed not to know. They knew the areas where they plied
their trade and maps were of no significance to them. But I had
seen large foreign-going cargo boats down the Amazon; surely
they would have charts? The Amazon is almost 4000 miles
long with over a thousand tributaries, eight of which are
themselves over a thousand miles long; I did not intend getting
lost in that lot without maps.

There is nothing like the Amazon, the largest volume of
fresh water in the world with a network of waterways extend-

ing millions of miles, its luxuriant forests are responsible for replenishing half the world's oxygen, and of the 22,000 known species of plants in the world, 18,000 of them can be found in the Amazon Basin.

I would spend hours at a time just gazing at the river, watching its titanic forces at work. Whirlpools, capable of causing serious handling difficulties to even the largest of ships, would form without warning. Different coloured rivers collided into it and ran parallel for miles without mixing. Boil-ups would occur seemingly without reason on calm and flat stretches of water. Yes, there were hazards, but it could be done.

I had seen jaguars caught in the area; I had little doubt there would be crocodiles, snakes and a host of other potentially dangerous animals. And yet the natives seemed to survive all right; or was it perhaps that they accepted a high mortality rate as normal?

I questioned crew members whenever I saw strange fruits, nuts or berries. Could they be eaten and how were they prepared? Large turtles were in abundance, in fact most of the food served on board these vessels was turtle meat. It was quite normal to find a live one kept in a closet for future supplies. On larger ships they were kept in the shower room, and if you did not want your toes bitten off whilst taking a shower, then it was necessary to keep stepping over them as they moved towards you. How they were caught, I did not know; in any case it would be a precarious business trying to haul one into a canoe. Fishing was, of course, a strong possibility if food supplies ran short. It would just be a question of identifying the edible species.

Towards the end of my trip, proceeding from Santarém to Belém, we ran into a violent tropical storm. Within minutes, the river changed from glassy calm to a raging sea. Rain reduced visibility to zero and the normal method of night navigation by spotlight was useless under these conditions. The order to stop engines came too late and soon we were aground in a swamp. The river was wide here, approximately six miles, and efforts to attract the attention of passing ships were unsuccessful. Swarms of mosquitos now attacked us relentlessly and I spent the night under a dirty tarpaulin.

There were some valuable lessons to be learnt; the speed with which conditions changed, the millions of mosquitos, and the dangers of night navigation. Also, if this 500-ton cargo boat was having difficulty in attracting attention, what chances would I have of being spotted under similar conditions in a canoe?

Next morning, a clear day, I had a good look over the ship. It was a sturdy old vessel and did not appear damaged. Getting it afloat again would be the only problem. The wheelhouse was very basic, no compass, no emergency equipment and, of course, no charts. I produced a large scale map of South America (approximately 100 miles to the inch) and asked the crew to estimate where we were. It soon became obvious that they had no experience whatsoever in using maps. It is very possible that many had never seen a map of the Amazon river before. They knew the sections they worked from memory and it was not necessary to know more.

We spent the morning trying to rock the boat free using great logs as levers while the engines were driven full astern. It was all in vain. We were hard aground and it would need a tow from a larger vessel. The crew gave up and spent the day fishing. The following day, a motorised canoe passed close enough for us to attract its attention. The captain did a deal with the owner to take him to the next major town where he could request assistance.

Just after midnight, the captain was back with a heavy cargo vessel to pull us free. A line was connected and the engines of both vessels driven full bore. A lot of vibration, a bit of rocking and swaying, but we were going nowhere. After twenty minutes, it was decided to call it off. Our vessel would have to be completely unloaded before anything more could be done. Since the other boat was going to Belém, the captain suggested I go with it as there was no telling how long he would be stuck.

I continued to take notes, reasonably happy about everything I had seen so far and confident that I could handle it OK. I'd bring an automatic shotgun for protection and I felt sure I would be able to get charts of the area. But how about the upper 2000 miles of the Amazon from its source in the Andes to Leticia? I knew there were two major towns on the river: Pucallpa and Iquitos, but between them or beyond them I knew nothing. Even the travellers' bible, *The South American Handbook*, gave no information on this region. I would write to missionaries working in this region. I had time. From Belém, I took a bus south to Brasilia, Rio and São Paulo, forever searching stores for books and maps. I obtained a copy of a then unpublished book on the main tributaries of the Amazon, giving times of year for maximum and minimum water levels and depths and, little by little, I gathered charts and maps of the lower reaches. But what of the upper reaches? I travelled through Uruguay, Paraguay, Bolivia and on to Peru. In the department of Cuzco I visited the famous Inca ruins of Machu Picchu. From this altitude (7500 feet) I could view a small stretch of the foaming, boiling Alto Urubamba, a headstream of the Ucayali, the prime tributary of the Amazon, described as impassable to all. Was it like this all the year or would it attenuate enough to get a canoe and perhaps six months' supplies and equipment through? There was no road for me to go down to check. What lay beyond the hairpin bends, waterfalls? That water would be icy cold, I would need a wetsuit and some warm woollen clothes for camping at night in this altitude. More weight, more cargo space needed; how big would the canoe have to be?

I travelled on to Nazca to see the famous figures of animals and geometric figures carved into the plain which are described as runways in Eric von Daniken's *Chariots of the Gods* but believed by others to be a giant calendar. Virtually unidentifiable at ground level, I hired a small plane to view them from 3000 feet. They were so beautifully clear from up above that I was tempted to hire another plane to view and photograph all the unknown sections of the Amazon, but such thoughts would take me well beyond my bank balance.

Two days later, I reached Lima and started my enquiries for maps of the upper reaches. The best available were 1:1,800,000; not much use for fine detail and river navigation but it was a good start. I got maps for the districts of Cuzco and Loreto and, crude as they were, they at least covered all the unknown areas.

I now relaxed for a week in Lima and, in between a cheerful girlfriend and an earth tremor that nearly brought the hotel roof on top of us, I continued to design my canoe and equipment. My next stops were Guatemala, Mexico, the USA and then on to London to see my son. At every opportunity I browsed around sports shops, camping stores and ships' chandlers, just on the off-chance I might spot something I could make use of on the trip. I never revealed my plans to anyone. Talking too much about anything is likely to do more harm than good and I was a strong believer in fate. In any case, I would only be told that I was potty for planning to canoe down the Amazon.

2 SEARCH FOR INFORMATION

Back in Australia, in July 1979, I started to compile a list of possible contacts for information on the unknown upper reaches of the Amazon. I visited travel agents in Sydney, claiming to be specialists in South America, but it only took me a few minutes to ascertain that I knew more about the area than they did. I contacted various religious organisations to find out if they had any missionaries operating in this region and received one or two hopeful contacts here. Finally, I received the name of a tour company in South America who organised rafting trips on sections of the Alto Urubamba. I was very optimistic until I received their brochure. The rafting trips were on the quieter stretches of the river, describing the areas beyond as 'impassable to all'. That kind of statement never left a glimmer of hope. But I was going to make this trip, come what may; nothing was impossible. It was just a matter of finding a way around, through or over the obstacles.

I read all I could but found most books to be grossly exaggerated adventure stories. I think the authors relied on the fact that few people would ever check their stories out. Some would have you believe there was a snake in every tree, a jaguar behind every bush, a shower of poison blowdarts from every village and, of course, the countless starving crocodiles and piranhas just waiting for a meal!

Working in the RAAF Instrument Laboratories gave me the opportunity to make and experiment with gadgets I would need. Batteries would be hard to come by for much of the trip and I would need them for my flashlamp, cameras and for the electronic mosquito repeller I was inventing, so I created a solar-powered battery charger.

The charger worked well, so I weatherproofed it and left it on the roof of my flat for further tests. To get the correct frequency for the mosquito repeller, I conducted a series of experiments. Apparently it is only the pregnant female mosquitos that bite you and so I had to find the frequency that disturbed them the most. One school of thought claims that 22kHz is the frequency used by the male mosquito for his mating call and at this frequency pregnant females will disappear from the scene. Even with my good eyesight, it was rather hard to spot the difference between males and females. So I caught whole batches of them in transparent plastic jars and used signal generators to try out the frequencies. There was indeed a noticeable twitching and irritation at the 22kHz mark, so I adjusted the repeller to this frequency and installed it in my flat. I left it running for months on end and there was a marked decline in mosquito bites. However, it was far from perfect.

I wrote to as many canoe manufacturers as possible, trying to locate the ideal model for the trip. My brother in England sent me catalogues and brochures of most types available there. The nearer I could get to my ideal canoe the fewer adjustments I would have to make. Without experience in fibreglassing or boat-building, I considered it wiser to buy a proven model and modify it to my requirements.

I frequently hired or borrowed canoes making notes of all their good and bad points, their stability, cargo capacity, windage, handling characteristics and comfort. Inflatable canoes looked good for a while; portability was a big point in their favour. However, I read various accounts of people being shipwrecked and having to spend three to four months in inflatable life rafts which soon began to disintegrate. It didn't look likely that they would last for the six months I would be under the tropical sun.

I would need a fairly large canoe both for supplies and also because I would probably have to sleep in it when I was unable to find a suitable landing spot. Many of the areas I had seen had trees and scrub far out from the banks, so it might be a question of finding a quiet spot and tying the canoe up to a tree. But then came the question of stability. A Canadian canoe seemed ideal; they had a large cargo capacity and would be big enough and stable enough to lie down and sleep in. But large Canadian canoes are not really suitable for a one-man expedition. Their extra weight and bulk would make them difficult to handle in white water and their high sides above the water line increased the windage.

Winds in the Amazon would come at me from either the north-east or the south-east and would always be adverse, slowing me down. But I would have to keep ploughing steadily into them however strong they were as I had to make the whole journey within the dry season. Canoeing in the wet season would be hell, for when it rains in the Amazon, the heavens really open. River levels rise by over fifty feet, the width changes from one to thirty miles, thousands of trees are uprooted and dragged along by the mainstream. Even the largest vessels cease to function under these conditions.

Perhaps a kayak would be more suitable but the smaller ones lacked the cargo capacity and the larger tourer and sea kayaks lacked the turning abilities essential in white water.

There are three basic types of kayak — the slalom, tourer and sea kayak. The slalom is a low capacity kayak, around thirteen feet long, very manoeuvrable and ideally suited to white water. The tourer, a higher capacity kayak around fifteen feet, is very directional and best on flat water, while the sea kayak is a high capacity kayak around eighteen feet, very directional and is, as its name implies, suited to ocean conditions.

My problem was that I needed a kayak with a reasonable cargo capacity which could handle white water, flat water and ocean conditions, and be stable enough to sleep in. On the last point, since a kayak has none of the stability associated with the wide-beamed Canadians, I toyed with the idea of having some form of quickly attachable outriggers that could improve stability enough for sleeping.

I made a rough assessment of cargo needed and estimated my barest minimum would weigh at least forty kilograms. It was easy to assess spare clothes, spare paddles, cooking pots, tent and sleeping-bag but knowing how much food to take was more complicated. For example I might reach a sizeable village every twenty days, but supposing they only had perishable goods to sell, like eggs, meat and fruit? How long would they keep in a kayak under the tropical sun? Perhaps another three days, and the next supply point might be twenty days on. Also how many kilos of repair material should I take? Enough for the whole trip or was there a possibility of supplies in the larger towns? How many shotgun shells was I likely to get through during the first month and how long before I could replenish my stock? So things invariably led back to finding more information on the area I was going to and that information was hard to come by.

In selecting equipment it was necessary to take into consideration every conceivable mishap or condition I was likely to encounter and how I could compensate for them. Supposing I was badly holed miles from anywhere? How would I get to the next place or village suitable for carrying out repairs? Somehow the canoe must be made to float with full cargo – including myself – even when flooded. Part of the answer was to have all the cargo in watertight containers or sealable air bags and to fill all spare cargo areas with the highly buoyant polystyrene foam. But it would still have to be kept stable and manoeuvrable.

The usual method of fixing a holed fibreglass canoe is to get it to the nearest bank by rowing (if you are lucky) or, more typically, swimming along with it and then either taping it up (emergency repair), or re-fibreglassing the damaged area. But it might be fifty miles before I found a suitable bank on the Amazon and then I might have to share it with a crocodile. A couple of easily attachable, inflatable outriggers seemed to be the answer, for emergencies as well as night-time stability.

I continually improved my knowledge of survival skills as I had good reason to believe I would need them. The RAAF had many films on this subject and I never missed an opportunity to see them, even if it meant suggesting to my superiors that we should have them for continuation training.

Books were another good source of survival techniques. It was important to know the mental attitude of those who had survived against incredible odds. Some were strong-willed people who had refused to give in to hopelessness and despair, many were deeply religious, while others had mentally trained themselves to react positively under such conditions. I decided the latter was more my line. I tried to imagine every conceivable mishap that could happen to me and worked out the most logical course of action to take in each case, how I should behave, what I should do, and what I should not do.

It should not be difficult to survive in the Amazon which possessed a quarter of the world's fresh water reserves, and over 1500 of the world's known 2000 species of fish. I would include some fishing line in my emergency kit. If my canoe was damaged beyond repair, I would make a raft. So long as I had some rope and a means of cutting the wood it should not be too difficult.

Getting bitten by a snake would, however, be a very serious problem. Being able to identify every poisonous snake and carrying anti-venom serum for all of them would not be feasible. I would have to rely on the basic method of using a tourniquet and cleaning the wound as best I could. A shotgun, used at close range, should protect me against the jaguars and crocodiles. I could also use the gun for killing wild pigs and other game. There should be no reason to go hungry.

Even at this stage, I did not visualise my journey as just another canoe trip: it would be every bit as much an exercise in survival. This gave it an extra dimension and made it more exciting and challenging.

Little by little, more information trickled in from South America. Some of my letters had been forwarded to the South American Explorers' Club (SAEC). The president of the SAEC, Tom Jackson, a keen canoeing and rafting enthusiast himself, answered many of my questions about the white-water tributaries high up in the Andes. Tom had been through some of the most dangerous areas on an inflatable raft and was able to give me good, if somewhat frightening, descriptions. It was impossible to examine many areas in advance and conditions could change abruptly from nothing to a deathtrap, without any warning because there was no way of obtaining information on any of the feeder streams coming down from the mountains. There were also huge whirlpools many feet across. (I was later to see photos of one of these in a club magazine.) The good news was that it could be done and that was something to be elated about in itself.

I joined the SAEC and continued a dialogue with Tom, though I didn't explain my full intentions, beyond saying that I intended setting out on a canoeing expedition from the district of Cuzco on to the lower reaches of the Amazon. I always avoided questions like, "How many people on your expedition?" as I feared a break in communication. Canoe clubs tend to frown on the one-man expeditions and it was very likely the Explorers' Club would. I was told there was a fair-sized town,

Atalaya, about ten days by canoe from Cuzco, that there were no maps of the area and no fibreglass materials available in Peru. Since I had already obtained maps of the area, I gathered what was meant was that there were no 'detailed' maps or charts suitable for navigational purposes. However, I was grateful for the information.

I photostatted the maps I had and sent a copy to the club, asking them to mark the main rapids and danger spots. It came as a bit of a shock to me when the Explorers' Club wrote back asking, "Where did you get those maps?" They were readily available just a short bus ride from the club's premises in Lima. I think I had located the source and purchased the maps within half a day of arriving there.

I do not wish to knock the club, because it is doing a fantastic job. It is non-profit-making, non-religious and non-political. It took a lot of hard work to get it going and it is an excellent place to meet and share experiences with fellow expeditionaries. But I have been travelling for about twenty years, have visited between sixty and seventy countries, many of them repeatedly, have seldom learnt more than a few words of any language and yet I have always managed to get what I need and go where I want. To me it is a question of being logical.

The next problem was how to get a kayak from Australia to Peru. I chased around the various shipping lines in Sydney and things did not look good. There was very little shipping between Australia and Peru and even scheduled trips would be cancelled if there was insufficient cargo to make them economical.

I tried the various airlines and received estimates ranging from $A200 to $A3000. I decided that someone must be getting their figures wrong and wrote to the senior cargo managers of the various airlines, giving full dimensions and weight. The figures I gave were of the maximum sized canoe I would take. Large capacity things like canoes do not get charged purely on weight. There is a formula whereby the sum of the linear dimensions is first taken, a certain rate figure is extracted from this, which is then multiplied by the actual weight. Qantas Airlines' senior cargo manager was most helpful but most other airlines either proved unhelpful or flatly refused to consider a canoe as they said it would not fit into their containers.

Considerable savings could be made by cutting the canoe in sections and rejoining it in Peru. This was fine, except the Explorers' Club had already informed me that no fibreglass repair materials were available in Peru and airline regulations and conditions concerning transportation of highly inflammable fibreglass resins were strict. Moreover the hardener or catalyst used with the resins is a lethal substance, capable of seeping out of any container you cared to put it in. All aircraft flying into or out of the USA were virtually banned from carrying the substance, and I would be passing through the USA on my way to Peru. But even if I never cut the canoe up, I would still need resins for my repairs. It was at times like this I had to visualise my goal and not the obstacles.

I wrote to the head office of the Australian post office explaining the situation, hoping they might be able to come up with something. I am still waiting for their reply. Next, I tried various resin manufacturers but none had experience of transporting their materials overseas. There would be a way, it was just to find it. I phoned the Peruvian consul about the availability of resins in South America. He was certain I would find them in Peru but could not say where. The SAEC was just as certain that I could not. I wrote to the British and Australian consuls in Peru, Brazil and other adjoining countries. If I could locate the stuff in South America it would save all the hassles and restrictions of trying to transport it from Australia. None of my letters were answered.

In April 1981, I had completed nine years' service with the RAAF and reluctantly decided to leave. I had enjoyed the RAAF; it was more than just a job. From a technical point of view, it had kept up with modern developments and in many ways had been a most challenging way of life. Although military organisations often encourage people to take part in sporting events and expeditions, they would have had a heart attack if they had heard of mine: a canoe trip of almost 4000 miles through some of the world's remotest areas by someone who had never been more than thirty miles in any one trip in his life. Most of my canoeing had been alone so I would not even be able to produce certificates from competitions or clubs testifying to my abilities. However, I was convinced that I could do what I was setting out to do. I was fit and healthy, did not drink or smoke and kept a sensible diet. I had had considerable experience in travelling and knew how to get by under the roughest conditions. I enjoyed the outdoor life and loved a good challenge.

I decided my trip would start in July 1982. June was the end of the wet season in the Andes area, and it was logical to begin the trip about then, even though I still did not have all the information I required.

In June 1981 I bought a thirteen-foot-six-inch fibreglass general purpose touring kayak for $A300. It had a two-foot beam and a red and white gel-coat finish. It had enough turning abilities to handle a moderate amount of white water, and on the flat water it would be in its element. Also, with a few minor modifications, it could be made to handle ocean conditions. Its capacity was 110 kilos and since I was under seventy kilos, that left a fair margin for cargo, so it seemed fairly close to my ideal.

3   GLADSTONE, THE PROVING GROUND

In July 1981 I moved to the coastal town of Gladstone in Queensland, a thousand miles north of Sydney. I had got a job as an instrument fitter at the world's largest alumina refinery. Gladstone was a boom town, the fastest growing in Australia, and I worked all the overtime I was offered. I had a reputation for never saying no. I had estimated the expedition would cost around $A5000 and I would need all the money I could get.

The other great advantage was that the area was an ideal training ground for my trip. The climate was sub-tropical, there were two tidal rivers, mangrove swamps, tidal rapids and, of course, the ocean.

When I first arrived in Gladstone I had a room with a family who made me feel really at home and often invited me to join them for a meal. The man of the house, Ivan, was of Yugoslav origin and had been a bit of an adventurer himself. About twenty years ago, when it had still been legal to shoot crocodiles in Australia, he had netted a small fortune hunting them in all the small coastal creeks. Twice bitten by snakes and once by a wounded crocodile, he was well worth listening to. One of the snakes had crept into his sleeping-bag at night, probably for warmth, and bit him as he tried to jump clear of it. That cost him six weeks of suffering in hospital. The crocodile that attacked him was one he had wounded and had not been quick enough reloading his gun. The result was some nasty gashes on the hands, but nothing too serious. "If they are under six feet, they don't usually attack you," he said. That was something I was to hear and read about again before my expedition.

Ivan had actually visited the Amazon area himself when restrictions on crocodile shooting had been imposed in Australia. After assessing some of the creeks and rivers, he had decided there was a fortune to be made in South America. It was just a question of getting a permit. The problem was that a small group of people with the right network of contacts controlled the market and did not intend letting anyone else in on it. Even an offer of $A7000 for a one-month permit could not persuade them. Having that many crocodiles in the area might have been good news to people like Ivan. However, it was anything but good news to me.

Nice as the family was, I needed somewhere I could formulate my plans and carry out the modifications to my kayak. Six weeks after reaching Gladstone, I bought a second-hand caravan and moved in. I also had a sixteen-foot annexe which acted as my workshop.

The first experiments I did were cargo capacity. I would find a quiet spot on the river, load the kayak up with thirty to forty kilos of sand and put it through its paces. Apart from the expected increase in load on the paddle, performance was not impaired. This was a good point. Many kayaks are designed for one weight only and any significant deviation from this will cause a drastic change in handling characteristics.

Distribution of the weight was another important factor, for both efficiency and safety. Too much weight in the stern and my kayak would waddle like a duck. Too much in the bow and it would nosedive. Too much in the nose and stern (i.e. not distributed evenly throughout its length) and it would rock or see-saw.

I also practised the usual one-man rescues; I would roll out of the kayak in midstream, then drain the cockpit and climb back in. This is fairly easy on most kayaks but I wanted as much familiarity with this particular model as possible.

Most of my kayaking was done at weekends and, as Christmas approached, the twelve-foot tides became more common. This, combined with a few heavy downpours, gave me the kind of action I was looking for. I would wait till the tide had peaked and turned and then canoe up and down the rapids until the flow got too strong to reach the top. I would then select the area of maximum flow and turbulence, face the kayak upstream and battle with it for as long as I could. It was good physical exercise and also good for concentration. The moment I relaxed, I would be rolled.

Whenever this happened, I would make my way to the bank and analyse the error I had made. Was it a careless stroke, a miscalculation, or did I just get too complacent? It did not matter here. Beyond the rapid was a long stretch of flat water and beaches that were easy to get to. But the Amazon was going to be different – the first mistake might be the last. I decided from then on I would be playing for real. No more screw-ups.

I did the occasional distance trip, usually only around thirty miles. I was not going in for any fanatical training programme. I had kept fairly fit all my life and, in my opinion, there were too many people jogging and training every day just to compensate for their over-eating, drinking and smoking. I could paddle thirty miles any day I chose, upstream or downstream, and it had very little effect on me.

I worked much of the Christmas period, only taking the odd day off to do a bit of canoeing. Everything was on schedule. Information continued to trickle in and I was content with progress. I still never mentioned my intentions to anyone, but I think some of those I worked with doubted that Gladstone was my destiny. I was often seen in ships' chandlers buying bits and pieces that were not normally associated with canoeing. Or I would be spotted on the river with some strange gadget on my kayak that would be rather difficult to explain away. Worse still, I would be seen getting maps photocopied of strange places that were not even vaguely connected with Gladstone (or Australia, for that matter).

Gladstone was essentially a company town with subsidised housing for married employees and their families. If one intended to settle down there, it was logical to be married and fit into the community. My well-meaning supervisor frequently played at match-maker, keeping me advised of what young ladies were in the market at the moment. I often wonder what he made of my lack of interest.

In the new year I assessed my funds and things looked pretty good. I should be able to sell my car and caravan for $A3000 which would be enough to get myself and the kayak to Peru. I already had a couple of thousand spare in the bank, which should cover the trip itself and, with six months to go before departure, I should be able to accumulate a small emergency fund.

I was still casting a fond eye on the big eighteen-foot sea kayaks, as they were the real expedition stuff. But lovely as they were, I didn't fancy taking one through some of the world's most dangerous white water. By keeping my present kayak, I could save a few hundred dollars. It had started to get a few chips and scratches from the rapids, but there was no structural damage. I might spend another $A200 modifying it with pump, hatches and compass, but I did not see any great expenses here. Cameras, binoculars, a strong waterproof watch, freeze-dried foods and camping equipment would absorb almost another $A1000. Over all, a little higher than my original estimate, but I would manage.

In March 1982, I got the modifications under way. The watertight compartments or hatches were very important. Apart from keeping the cargo dry, they also created extra buoyancy should the kayak get flooded. Each of the hatches (one in the bow and the other at the stern) had two covers, a small five-inch diameter screw-action type on deck, and a larger (approximately nine-inch diameter) aluminium-backed fibreglass cover, accessible from the cockpit area. These internal covers were secured in place by wing nuts.

The purpose of the small deck-mounted covers was for quick and easy access to emergency equipment and the more frequently used items such as food packs and cooking pots. The internal covers were for spare paddle blades, large plastic containers and the more bulky items not likely to be needed frequently.

I reasoned that the best place to keep personal documents and money would be as close to me as possible. And, since I would be wearing a buoyancy vest for most of the time, I would either buy one with pockets fitted or install concealed watertight pouches on the inside. As always, I did my shopping carefully. I would be wearing the vest for months on end and it would be of no use if it was uncomfortable or chafing and causing sores. I found a good one for $A40 and set to work stitching in the pouches inconspicuously below the armpits. A buoyancy vest is a compromise garment, more streamlined than a life-jacket, so that it doesn't impede the paddling action, but it will not save an unconscious wearer. It is merely a floatation aid.

Next to be fitted was the pump and compass. The pump was from Ireland and the compass from Finland. The kayak was already taking on an international appearance. The pump was a ten-gallon-a-minute, hand-operated diaphragm type, fairly essential equipment for the one-man rescue, and correct positioning was crucial. A pump mounted incorrectly can make re-entry into a kayak somewhere between difficult and impossible. The normal method of getting back into a kayak is over the stern: with legs astride the kayak, you pull yourself over the surface and up to the cockpit area. The rear deck just behind the cockpit area is also the ideal place to fit the pump so that it can be operated whilst sitting in the cockpit. However, a pump handle sticking out between your legs can make re-entry into the cockpit very difficult. I put my pump just behind the cockpit within easy reach of my right hand and, importantly, almost flush with the deck.

What I needed next was a detachable fin on the stern and a detachable wave-deflector for the bow, both made from fibreglass. The fin would improve directional stability on the flat water stretches, and the wave-deflector would assist the kayak in riding the ocean rollers as I approached the Amazon mouth.

I had purchased a cheap movie camera for the trip and decided to give it a trial on my next outing. I mounted the camera just forward of the cockpit, leaving my hands free for paddling. The idea proved successful on flat water, but of doubtful use amongst the roller waves. The varying intensity of the sun's reflections from the waves caused the light meter to oscillate and produce alternate batches of dark and light frames. However, I considered it useful enough for the trip and, at $A34, it would not be a financial disaster if I lost it.

The wave-deflector proved itself during ocean trials and the fin was excellent on the flat water.

Another of my letters enquiring about fibreglass resins had been forwarded to the SAEC in Lima and I got a reply from the new president, Linda Rosa. She had contacted everybody that might know and they had all advised the same. "Bring everything with you – no stocks locally." I had a small win from another angle, eucalyptus oil (a well-known mosquito repellent in Australia) was available in Lima. That was something else I would not have to take with me on the plane. It had a bad habit of seeping from containers and saturating your luggage.

I had loaned my electronic mosquito repeller to a work-mate for further tests. He was living on a yacht in a local creek and was being plagued by mosquitos. It was an ideal place to test it. But after weeks of tests, he was not sure if it was attracting or repelling them, so I decided to give it a miss and rely on the eucalyptus.

My next task was to fit the emergency outriggers or 'inflatable compensations', as I called them. I had purchased two inflatable reinforced plastic yacht fenders about three feet long and ten inches in diameter (when inflated). They could be rolled down quite small and secured with shock cord to eyelets along the sides of the kayak. If I got holed or needed a stable platform for sleeping, it was easy just to release and inflate them with the deck pump or by the mouth. I took the kayak out to midstream at the weekend, swamped it, released the compensators and inflated them whilst drifting downstream. A couple of minutes and I had a stable platform to climb on to. In fact, it was stable enough to stand upright in the flooded cockpit. Although I usually selected quiet spots to test equipment or practise my emergency drills, local farmers must have wondered sometimes what the hell I was doing as I filled the kayak with sand or water and rolled it over.

Another idea that came to mind was a small canopy that could be erected over the cockpit area. A mosquito net fitted over the top of this and I would have had a weatherproof, mosquito-proof sleeping area for places where the normal method of camping was not possible – swamplands, for example. But in trial this was less successful. It would be ideal on a bank or quiet spot out of wind, but with the slightest breeze it made the kayak unstable in the water.

The last batch of gadgets were a paddle park (to leave my hands free for map reading or other tasks), a two-litre drinking-water container fitted beside the seat, and a series of eyelets placed along the length of the deck. The eyelets were laced with shock cord and would allow spare paddles or maps to be secured to the deck.

I bought a small spring-balance with a hook so I could weigh things. Then I compiled two lists of cargo, giving different priorities to each. The indispensable list consisted of essential items like spare paddle blades, medicines, repair kit, maps, food and basic camping equipment. Cameras, binoculars, tent and sleeping-bag were on the lower priority list. Knowing how much space to allow for equipment unavailable in Gladstone was tricky; I could only estimate the size and weight of these items and insert something else in their place. For example, I knew the approximate size and weight 'of one packet of freeze-dried food, but could only make a rough estimate of the area needed for a hundred packs. The packs varied in bulk according to their contents and could not be fitted in neat little rows. As some of these unavailable items were essential, it made it doubly difficult to assess likely space left over for low priority objects.

A spare paddle and perhaps one or two more rugged items could be secured on deck. However, there were great limitations here; deck cargo had a bad habit of getting torn free in white water.

I had two types of paddles for the trip. One was of a hard plastic material, virtually unbreakable and well suited to the white-water regions. The other was a lightweight all-fibreglass paddle, ideally suited to distance touring. I would also get some spare blades made up. It was difficult to predict how many I could get through in 4000 miles. Breakage and loss would be the biggest problem, but a trip of that distance might wear a blade or two out.

Tents were out and so were sleeping-bags, wet suits and warm clothes. Most of the trip would be through the tropics and I could use a poncho or space blanket as protection from the weather. Also I could light fires to keep warm at night. The gun was going to be a tricky point. It would have to be kept both easily accessible and at the same time dry. This implied keeping it in some kind of waterproof pouch inside the cockpit. I had not yet purchased a gun as I was going to leave that till I reached Sydney.

There was not too much else to test now. I just needed to become as familiar with the equipment as possible, make a few trips and simulate a few mishaps.

By June, it was close enough to take off to get my vaccinations up to date and my medical kit organised. My smallpox and yellow fever were still current and so tetanus and cholera injections were all that I needed. I also got a prescription for some antibiotics, anti-malaria and dysentery tablets. Added to these would be the non-prescription drugs such as aspirin and salt tablets. Not a very impressive array but, like everything else, it was the barest of essentials, the narrowest of margins. For water purification, I had some iodine-based tablets supplied by the airforce – I had exaggerated my need for them on a previous overseas trip.

I handed my notice in at the refinery and told them my intentions. As expected, I was swamped with advice and encouragement by the self-proclaimed experts. "You won't get a hundred miles"; "The piranhas will have you"; "A blowdart in the neck"; "Dead within a week". This was one of the reasons why I had never mentioned my expedition to anyone before. I fully anticipated an abundance of advice from people who had seen the spiced-up documentaries on TV. Another reason was that over-advertising is like over-planning: it tempts fate and things go wrong.

The Falklands/Malvinas dispute worried me. I never doubted that Britain would settle it quickly but how long resentment and possible travel restrictions on British subjects lasted in South America was less predictable. I was of dual nationality, British and Australian, so could use either passport, but there were certain advantages in using a British passport in South America because British citizens did not require visas for Peru or Brazil, whereas Australians did. Visas only lasted three months from date of issue and, since I might take longer than that to reach the Brazilian border, the visa might have expired before I got there. The thought of having to leave the kayak at the border while I travelled to, say, Rio for a visa extension decided me to risk travelling on my British passport.

By mid-June, the main outstanding issue was fibreglass resins: could I fly them into South America or obtain them locally? I contacted Ciba Geigy, the multinational plastics firm, to see what they knew. I was delighted when I received their reply. Branches in Peru and Brazil almost certainly produced resins similar to those I required. I made a phone call to the company's Sydney branch to get the types and numbers of compatible resins and then contacted the Peruvian office. They had what I wanted – another breakthrough. The Peruvian branch was in Lima, not far from the Explorers' Club.

I received a letter from *Guinness Superlatives* (*The Guinness*

Book of Records) in reply to my enquiry as to the estimated distance I would be canoeing along the Amazon river. Since the Amazon was being remeasured, they referred me to the National Geographical Society of the USA. I was to receive their reply in Lima.

I wrote to my brother and son in England, informing them of my intentions. If they were really quick, they could write back and advise me against it. However, I doubted that postal services were that good.

The question of guns was still unsettled. I had spent many hours pondering the pros and cons. Keeping a gun and ammunition both rapidly accessible and dry, would be difficult. The amount of time needed to dismantle, dry and clean a gun every day would be unacceptable. There were, of course, other angles to consider apart from the wild animals. I anticipated the odd encounter with thieves and robbers and a gun would be excellent protection. But supposing after days of hard going with very little sleep, somebody tried to hassle me or kept prowling around my camp out of curiosity? When you are tired and irritable, that is when you make mistakes, and squeezing a trigger is one of the easiest. South American jails are not very pleasant and doing a stretch in one did not appeal to me. I was ninety per cent sure at this stage that guns were out.

One of the last exercises I conducted with my kayak was night navigation. I paddled about fifteen miles downstream and sat on a bank for a snack before nightfall. When it was dark enough, I started back upstream. The first hour was fine, with just enough light to make out the profile of the banks. By the second hour, things changed dramatically; the sky blackened and not so much as a glint of starlight could be seen. With no movement on the water (it was getting close to high tide), I had no idea which way I was facing. I found one of the banks, re-established my bearings, and followed it as closely as possible, occasionally bumping into over-hanging branches. Schools of startled fish would dart in all directions, many jumping clear of the water, hitting the kayak and, in one case, landing on my spray cover. He was only a little fellow but the lesson was valuable. If I had not had the spray cover on, he would now be flipping about in the cockpit. Supposing he had been a bit bigger or more teethy, like the piranha? There is very little room to manoeuvre your legs in the cockpit of a kayak and any attempt to get them clear of a snapping fish could easily result in capsizing and joining the rest of the school in the river.

A mile or so further upstream, I spotted a lamp on the side of the river, almost certainly that of a night fisherman. It was a useful marker in an otherwise blackened environment. As I approached, I realised that it was a dad lecturing his kids on too much talking and not enough concentration on their fishing. If he had done less talking, they would probably have heard me approaching. I was within about twenty feet of them before they spotted the white sides of my kayak reflecting the light of their lamp. Mum gave a startled gasp as I passed by. She must have thought it was a great white pointer from the *Jaws* movie come upstream for a meal! After checking me out with a hand lamp, they went quickly back to fishing, their senses a little sharpened.

Fortunately, the tide had peaked by the time I reached the most rocky area on the river. I cleared the lot without the slightest bump or scrape. That was pure luck and very little to do with judgement. I seldom got through this section, even in broad daylight, without a few scrapes from the oyster-covered rocks below the surface.

By the third week in June, I decided it was time to get the kayak cleaned up and ready for the trip. I sanded it back and painted it over with polyester resin. Owing to all my modifications and adjustments, the weight had increased from eighteen to twenty-three kilos. This would mean five kilos less cargo could be carried, but the modifications had been essential.

I cut the fibreglass touring paddle into two sections for transportation and removed the blades of the white-water paddle from their aluminium shaft. I sold my caravan, my television and most other bits and pieces I would not be taking with me. Earlier in the year I had been the innocent party in two traffic accidents in two weeks. At the time I had wondered if someone, somewhere, was trying to tell me something. The insurance company had written my car off but allowed me to keep the salvage for a $A500 deduction from the final settlement figure. Mechanically, it was still sound and would be ideal for getting all my equipment to Sydney. By 12th July there was nothing left for me to do in Gladstone. I lock-wired the nearside doors of my car to prevent them falling off, lashed my kayak to the roof and set off.

My flight was booked for 21st July to Los Angeles where I would have to spend two days, before taking a connecting flight to Lima. A small problem was showing its head here; Qantas had agreed to take the kayak as excess baggage to Los Angeles for $A400 but the only response from the South American airline, Varig, was to quote the excess baggate rates for the kayak without actually specifying that they would take it. The travel agents told me not to worry as at least it would get to Los Angeles OK. My reply to this was that a kayak in Los Angeles Airport was of no more use to me than a kayak in Gladstone, in fact it might turn out to be a lot more expensive with airport charges. I put some pressure on them to get better results.

The travel agents had sent a few telexes off trying to get positive answers for me but the best they could come up with was, "When you get to Los Angeles, ask for Jerry – he knows about it." There were only eleven million people in Los Angeles and I guess everybody knew Jerry.

My first job in Sydney was to try and obtain letters of introduction from the Brazilian and Peruvian consulates, explaining the purpose of my trip. Countries with military governments are renowned for their document-mindedness. The Peruvian consulate suggested that I get letters from canoeing organisations establishing who I was; as far as he was concerned, I might be taking a canoe full of cocaine to Peru. I thought this was a reasonable argument but, being a loner, I would be hard pressed to find anybody in the canoeing fraternity who had even vaguely heard of me. The Brazilian consul did everything to try to dissuade me from even setting out, telling me how many people vanished in the Amazon area every year. I eventually extracted a reluctant letter from the Peruvian consul. The Brazilian said he would get me something typed up in the next day or so and post it on to me. That was one letter I knew I would not be getting.

My other jobs in Sydney involved trying to convince American Express to give me a credit card. (They did!) A plastic card could get me home even if all my money rotted away. I also needed two miscellaneous charges orders (MCOs) for further air travel. Many countries, Peru included, require an air ticket out before they let you in, but will accept an MCO of suitable denomination instead. There was very little point in buying an air ticket out of Peru since I intended to leave that country by kayak.

Sydney was also the place to stock up on freeze-dried foods. I had contemplated taking enough for several months, but when I saw how bulky just forty-four packs were, I knew I would have to rely on being able to buy food from the local Indians. Safety margins were getting thinner all the time. To be on the safe side in another respect I purchased four kilos of epoxy resin from Ciba Geigy's Sydney branch. If by some twist of fate the Peruvian branch had sold out by the time I arrived, I would be in a nasty predicament. Epoxy resins cost three times as much as polyester resins but are more acceptable to the aviation industry as they are non-flammable and referred to as 'safe' throughout the plastics industry. The catalyst or hardener was also referred to as 'safe', but I decided against taking any of that with me in case I upset some airline official. Instead I telephoned Peru to double check that they had some hardener in stock.

On the twenty-first I set off with my kayak wrapped in protective bubble paper and all my gear in three bags. My cousin Teresa escorted me to the airport and asked if she should report me missing after not hearing from me for a couple of months. I explained that it could take six months before hearing anything from me and if I'd been missing for that long in the Amazon there would be little point in looking for me.

My first job on arriving in Los Angeles was to locate my kayak, which was too big for the conveyor system. A customs official got things organised for me and also located a hotel willing to accept both me and the kayak. It was going to cost me $65 a night, but it was hard to lug a kayak around town looking for something cheaper. The hotel staff locked it away in a spare baggage-room and I was unable to unwind a little. Stage one had been completed successfully.

On 22nd July, I had to return to the airport and find 'Jerry'.

Apparently, Jerry was in some way connected with the Brazilian airline, Varig. So I walked up to their front counter and asked if anyone there knew Jerry. "Yes, we will just get him for you," was the reply. Jerry came out, took one look at me and said, "You must be the guy taking a canoe to Peru. Just take it round to the cargo bay and ask for Eddy. He is expecting it."

Well, that had gone smoothly, so I returned to the hotel to collect the kayak feeling very cheerful, only to find that I was unable to open the baggage-room door sufficiently wide to get it out. Originally, it had been placed upright against the far wall, as it was too long to lie on the floor. Somehow, it had slipped and wedged itself between the far wall and the door. Perhaps it did not want to go down the Amazon after all! Various staff members tried in vain to get their arms far enough round the door to move the kayak clear. Finally, someone remembered that there was an exceptionally skinny Chinese waiter working in the hotel and set off to get him. With a few wriggles and twists, our Chinese friend was round the door. No damage to the kayak, so it was on to a taxi and off to the airport.

Next afternoon, 23rd July, I boarded Varig flight RG33 bound for Lima.

4   BACK TO PERU

I emerged from Lima Airport at nearly midnight and the beginning of the national Independence day holiday week. Not the best time to haggle with a taxi driver when also carrying three bags and a kayak. But at least the Peruvian consul's letter had been worth the hassle and helped me through customs.

The South America Explorers' Club premises were a spacious first floor apartment, walls covered with maps and photos. Club members embraced a broad range of activities, including mountaineering, bush trekking, river rafting, exploring and canoeing, and the membership had a strong contingent of North American expatriates. Now for the first time I explained the nature and purpose of my trip to Linda Rosa, the current club president, as I wanted her to write me a letter like the Peruvian consul's to add a tone of authority to the expedition. I was expecting ridicule or at least dire warnings and was surprised how calmly she took the enterprise.

Linda was one of the founding members of the SAEC and a nurse by profession. She had done some nursing in the jungle regions of Peru so her experiences were worth listening to. She told me that the African chigger can now be found in South America, in the long grass. Although they usually only bother cattle, they can burrow under human skin and cause extreme irritation. She'd had a chigger bite which had almost driven her crazy for the best part of a week. After unsuccessfully trying all known skin ointments, she finally came up with her own remedy of putting nail varnish over its breathing hole and suffocating it. Simple, but effective remedies like that were of the type I needed to know. I had some plastic glue in my repair kit and would use this should the need arise. She was also able to give me reliable brand names of medicated soap. I anticipated coming into contact with lots of biting and possibly infectious insects during the trip, so it would be wise to keep my skin as clean as possible.

Later in the day I was to meet another club member, John

Davy, who was a keen canoeist himself and was now running river-rafting trips on sections of the Urubamba. He took one look at my kayak and said, "Mmm. Not for white water, that one." I agreed, but told him of the compromises I had had to make to find something suitable for the entire trip. "Mmm," said John again, neither approving nor disapproving. "Things are picking up now; rains are on the increase from the mountains. Take some heavy-gauge fishing line with you. Very good for trading with the Indians." I thanked John for another little piece of useful information.

My resin worries were finally resolved when I was able to purchase the elusive hardener from Ciba Geigy. While at the Peruvian airline, Faucett, I was told there would be no problem in flying the kayak to Cuzco.

I was still wondering about taking a gun. My sole weapon at this stage was a sheath knife, stored at an accessible point in the cockpit. But I had seen a small ·22 calibre pistol in a downtown store and thought it would be useful against small animals like snakes and a good deterrent to robbers. Also, it would be easy to conceal in my buoyancy vest. I made some enquiries and was informed that it was almost impossible for non-residents to obtain pistol permits. Shotgun permits were a possibility, but it would take about three weeks. So that was the gun problem solved for me and, in a way, I was glad.

Still in quest of good up-to-date maps, I paid a visit to the Instituto Geografico Nacional. They had started gathering aerial photos of river sections between Pucallpa and Iquitos, but these turned out too expensive and too bulky for my purposes. I would have needed at least twenty.

I spent a lot of the holiday period shopping for items like oats and milk powder and endlessly arranging and rearranging the cargo. This was a real nightmare. I bought a fork and a spoon and cut most of the handles off so they would fit inside my small billy can. Occasionally other club members popped in for a chat and perhaps a word of warning on some area they had just passed through. The mountaineers said, "Don't trust your maps, you'll get lost. We're always finding mountains that are not on the charts." I was to hear this remark once too often to ignore it. Apparently local surveyors mark or plot all the visible peaks and valleys in a given area but if, through mist or bad weather, some parts are not visible then a certain amount of assumption and interpolation take place. I was not doing any mountain climbing but perhaps similar assumptions had been made on unobserved parts of rivers.

By Monday, 2nd August, the holiday period was over and most places were getting back to normal. I called on the Brazilian consul to ask for a letter of introduction, as approximately 2000 miles of my expedition would be through Brazilian territory. "Are you going to Iquitos?" asked the consul's assistant. "That would be the best place to get it." In Sydney they'd said apply in Lima. Now in Lima they said apply in Iquitos. I almost lost my cool. I told him what had happened in Sydney and what I knew would happen in Iquitos. "Mmm," he said. "Please take a seat for a moment."

Fifteen minutes later the consul appeared with a neatly typed letter. I was so elated; the best I had expected was the typical Latin response of *mañana* (tomorrow).

Finally, I called at the club to repack the cargo into my bags and rewrap the kayak ready for transportation to Cuzco. As I was leaving, I spotted two maps framed and hung high up on the wall. They covered the Amazon area from Cuzco to Iquitos and were double the scale of anything that I had for that region. I had been chasing larger maps for almost three years, being repeatedly told by the club that such things did not exist, and now here they were hanging on the club wall: they must have been there so long that they had taken on the appearance of wallpaper. The maps were updated editions of original aerial surveys carried out by the US Air Force in the sixties, printed in America. I started to trace them, but then decided to wait until the morrow and get the president's permission to photostat them.

When I looked at them closely next morning I had problems finding the point where the two maps overlapped; they did not seem to have anything in common. I then realised why. The survey for one had been done in the wet season and the other in the dry. It was impossible to believe that you were looking at the same river. New islands and channels had formed, while others had vanished. The river width on one map was three times that of the other and with no significant landmarks, it would be a navigational nightmare trying to work out where I was. Distances varied greatly too, depending on river width and which channels were open. I could measure up to five miles' difference on some bends. However, if used in conjunction with my other maps, I would hopefully be able to work out my position.

I purchased my air ticket to Cuzco and made one last check with the staff that there would be no problem in taking my kayak along with me. I gave them all the dimensions again and insisted they recheck with the cargo department. This they did and assured me that there would be no problems. My flight was for 0715 on Thursday, 5th August.

Linda had completed her tour of duty as club president and returned to the States. The new president was Elizabeth Mosczynski who was most helpful. I asked her if I could leave a bag of spare clothes in the club, which I would collect around Christmas time. Before she could answer, a pessimistic mountaineer told me not to worry, I would be dead in two months anyway and they would sort my things out for me. Not exactly the type of cheer I needed before setting out on a unique enterprise. Lisa also arranged an interview for me with the Lima *Times*. Although I never wanted publicity for my trip, it was advisable to have some to prove it wasn't a hoax. I would be staking a claim with the *Guinness Book of Records,* if I was successful, and they would need press coverage to prove that I really had been to the places I said I had.

Ann Reynolds of the Lima *Times* asked me the usual questions about my age, training, health, family background and canoeing experience. This last I was reluctant to answer for, in truth, I had never been on a longer trip than thirty miles and knew what spiced-up stories newspapers were capable of. 'Man who's never canoed more than thirty miles to attempt 4000 miles of Amazon' sounded like a possible headline. I cannot remember now what I told Ann but I know I was rather evasive.

I had another newspaper interview, with a freelance English journalist, Martin Trew. Martin was working for the *Sunday Times* and had stopped off at the club in anticipation of finding some adventurers. I showed him the kayak and equipment and explained the short-comings of the maps on the upper reaches of the Amazon. "What would you do if you were attacked by crocodiles?" he asked. It was one of those questions which is hard to answer. Unarmed and faced with death, you would undoubtedly try to put up some token resistance like striking it across the nose with a plastic paddle, but if it had decided it was going to have you, then you might be better off praying. Martin gave me a hand to get the kayak down to the street and on to the top of a combi van for delivery to the airport ready for tomorrow's flight.

"What's this for?" they asked me when I arrived at the cargo terminal. "It's going on tomorrow's flight to Cuzco," I said. "Not possible," they replied, "cargo bookings are full for a week." I got the cargo manager to contact their main office in town and speak to the lovely receptionist who had assured me there would be no problems. He spoke to her for a couple of minutes and then passed me the phone. "What is wrong?" I asked her. "Yesterday you assured me there'd be no problem in taking my kayak." "I must have spoken to a different cargo manager," replied the girl. "I don't know what went wrong." "Well, I need that kayak on tomorrow's flight. Now what can you do about it?" She gave me the name of a senior representative of the airline and recommended that I talk to him. "He's a very nice man," she added. With that, she put the phone down and washed her hands of the whole affair.

So, off I went from building to building, office to office; "Please talk to this man . . . please contact this lady . . . please see that man", a fine game of passing the buck. I kept at it for over an hour until I was ninety per cent convinced that something was being done. I then returned to the cargo area and spoke again with the cargo manager. He quietly and politely explained the problems of balancing the amount of cargo and number of passengers that could be taken on a flight. We then carried the kayak across the hall to get it weighed. I was prepared at this stage to say, "Look, if it costs double, I'll pay." The manager made a few calculations and without actually saying it was going, gave me a bill for excess baggage. It was no use asking for guarantees, verbal or otherwise, but I was quietly hopeful that the kayak would be on tomorrow's flight.

I returned to the club to find two letters: one from my

brother expressing his admiration for what I was doing but warning me to take care and mentioning the names of people who had vanished in the Amazon area and another from the National Geographical Society of the USA to say that they were in the process of remeasuring the Amazon so no distances could be given. My own estimate of the distance I would be travelling from Quiteni in the department of Cuzco in Peru to Cabo Maguari, Ilha Marajo in Brazil was approximately 3800 miles.

My last duties in Lima were to send a letter to the *Guinness Book of Records*, giving full details of my intentions and to cash another travellers' cheque to boost my supply of local currency. I did not anticipate finding too many places to cash travellers' cheques down the Amazon.

I rose early on 5th August. By 0530 I was at the airport. I spotted one of the senior airline staff and asked her if she knew anything of my kayak. She was not sure if it had been loaded on to the 0715 plane or not. So, in finest Gestapo style, I politely informed her of what would be written about her airline if the expedition failed due to any fault on their part. She never stopped running for the next fifteen minutes. At 0555 she returned to the counter, breathless, and asked if I minded going on the earlier 0600 flight as they had managed to get my kayak on that one. Off I went.

Landing in Cuzco shortly after 0700, I picked up my three bags and made for the cargo area. My luck was in; there was my kayak, sitting on the tarmac. I presented the excess baggage ticket to one of the ground staff and he gave me a hand with the kayak out to the taxi rank. With a sly grin he asked me if I was off to the Malvinas. That was the first mention of the islands I had heard since being in Peru.

On reaching the city, my first task was to find a bus going to Quillabamba, the last major town before Quiteni, my expedition starting point. However, I was told that the service had been suspended and advised to go by train. One of the trains going to Quillabamba had been cancelled and the other was for passengers only – no cargo. So I returned to the taxi to see what the driver knew. "There's some trucks going that way," he said. "They leave from the market." When we arrived there, we found one almost immediately. "Watch for the thieves," advised the driver, "the market's full of them." I replied that I knew, but thanked him anyway.

The truck driver wanted 7000 soles (approximately $A10) for a twelve-hour trip; not a bad price considering the amount of gear I had. For the next few hours, I sat under the blazing sun while sacks and baskets were loaded aboard. The sun was especially strong in Cuzco, with its high altitude (11,400 feet) and rarefied air. It is not unusual to have your skin burnt and peeling after one day in Cuzco and, if you step into the shadows, you will soon be shaking and shivering. By 1200 all the cargo was aboard, plus fifteen other passengers and one sheep. We were perching on knobbly vegetable sacks and hard angular baskets of fruit. Most of the passengers were sturdy market women of Indian descent, their language was the old Inca tongue, Quechua, with a sprinkling of Spanish which I found hard to follow.

The first part of the trip was interesting as we drove past many Inca ruins, but gradually the weather became overcast and the temperature plummetted. Frequent icy showers stung our faces in the back of the truck. When the rain became too heavy, we rolled a large tarpaulin over the top of us, each person hanging on to a side or corner to prevent it blowing away.

I bought some fruit at a wayside halt and shared it with all the passengers: they in turn gave me a few bits and pieces, perhaps a different fruit or a piece of bread. At most of the stop-offs, cooked food was on sale, just a small roadside cart with cooked rice, beans, fish or meat, but the general handling and hygiene left a lot to be desired so I never bothered with it. I had travelled like this before and knew that I could manage on fruit.

By evening, I was feeling pretty tired. A long bumpy ride with a sack of potatoes for a seat does tend to wear one down. Some of the market women continued to talk to me, but I didn't follow much of what they said; I just wanted to doze. I gave a few polite *no comprenders* and eventually they left me alone. The icy showers continued for the remainder of the trip making sleep impossible.

We reached Quillabamba at 0100 next morning and drove into the market-place. My fellow passengers hopped off and immediately began to prepare their goods for the next day's market. As soon as one day's selling stopped, new produce was trucked in and sorted for the next in an eternal round of activity. The driver asked me if I wanted to sleep in the truck until daylight, when I could organise a lift to Quiteni. Five of the market women also elected to stay in the truck which gave rise to much good-humoured banter, the driver saying he did not know if it was wise to leave one gringo and five senoritas together for the rest of the night. All the women laughed: either they did not anticipate any problems or possibly would welcome some.

I soon curled up on the floor of the truck to sleep despite the bitter cold. One of the market women dropped a blanket on top of me. I gave a hearty *muchas gracias* which brought a shower of laughter. I seemed to understand nothing unless there was something in it for me, so they branded me the "Gringo Opportunist".

About 0600 my truck driver took me to where a truck bound for Quiteni was loading. The driver wanted 10,000 soles, rather a large sum for a five-hour journey so I decided to have a quick scout around for something cheaper. I ate some more fruit but noticed I was now getting stomach problems which could be most inconvenient.

At 0800 an old bomb of a bus pulled down the side street and started taking on passengers. The driver wandered up and down the street looking for more business. He spotted me and asked where I was going. "Quiteni," I answered, "how about you?" "Yes, Quiteni," he replied. "How much?" "Two thousand eight hundred soles including luggage." Just what I wanted. There was a large roof rack, too, so no problem for the kayak.

Just before noon, with the bus packed to capacity and the inside like an oven, we got under way. The journey would be about five hours and only my worsening dysentery problem bothered me. All the windows were left wide open to try and keep things cool but this, unfortunately, allowed clouds of dust in from the unsealed road. Many of the passengers sat on the floor. I was under the impression that these people paid a lower fare than seated passengers, as most of them looked rather poor and never attempted to take a seat when a vacancy occurred. A couple of stops were made at roadside stalls but, hungry or not, I avoided them. Just a bottle of soft drink and a bit more fruit. Just before dusk we reached Quiteni.

Myriads of small shallow rivulets of water flow down from below the Andean snowline; at about 17,000 feet these begin to coalesce into slightly larger but still exceptionally fast flowing streams which gradually race together to form feeders for the Urubamba river which is a headstream of the Ucayali, the Amazon's prime tributary. It would be foolhardy to bring a fully laden kayak down the shallow, precipitous, boulder-strewn mountain streams so I was joining the river where its greater width and depth would allow me room to manoeuvre. I would still encounter severe conditions for I was at an altitude of 3000 feet with the much feared Pongo ahead of me, but as it was the dry season I did not anticipate any grade-six nightmares, although I hadn't promised myself anything easy.

Rivers are graded by canoeists into a numbered system from one to six depending on the degree of difficulty, severity of conditions, and the likely consequences of making a mistake. However, individual rapids or sections of a river may vary considerably in grades.

A grade one to two would be ideal for novices to cut their teeth on, small rapids and drops, and simple obstructions. Whereas a grade six is a definite threat to life, long, difficult and violent rapids, whirlpools, steep gradients, narrow passages and drops which only the most experienced canoeists should attempt. Taking a fully loaded kayak through a grade six was unthinkable.

The main part of the village was about half a mile from the Urubamba river and there was a clear running stream behind it. I booked into the only hotel, Quiteni Hotel, which offered dormitory-style accommodation at 750 soles per night – buy your own candle if you want to read or write after dark.

In the last light of the day, I went down to the river to make an assessment of conditions. It was indeed a powerful river; fast-running with a grade-three rapid nearby. The water was clear and cold with large rocks and pebbles forming the beaches. I considered it wise to spend another day or two solving the cargo problem as there was no room for error here.

After a good wash and clean up in the stream behind the hotel, I ordered a meal of rice and meat. Then I took my first Maloprin anti-malarial tablet and made a note of this in my log. I must remember to repeat the dosage on the same day of every week for the whole of my expedition for malaria was rampant in the Amazon.

Next day I moved into a large double room owned by Herman Manga, the local pharmacist. I still had dysentery which was a nuisance, particularly when I had to make a dash into the trees in the middle of the night. The deadly bushmaster snake was active in these parts so I had to be careful where I squatted down.

I spent the morning unwrapping the kayak and refitting the peripheral items removed for transporting: the paddle park, pump handle and water outlet pipe. Then I joined Señor Manga and his family for lunch. I asked what they knew about whirlpools in the Pongo Mainiqui area.

Pongo means narrow and Mainiqui means gateway, for this is where the river shrinks to one-third of its width as it cuts through sheer granite cliffs. Portaging is impossible. Tom Jackson had been the first to warn me of this place saying that it could be nothing or a deathtrap, depending on the level of the river at the time I went through, which varied on a daily basis depending on the weather high up in the Andes. Señor Manga murmured about whirlpools but was more interested in what I would do when I reached Pucallpa, the first major town on the river. "Will you then go home to Australia?" "No, I'll continue on to Iquitos," I said.

"Then will you return to your home?"

"No, I'll continue on to Brazil."

This was something I did not like discussing. When you tell people you intend to travel thousands of miles with such basic equipment, they start to look at each other in disbelief.

After lunch, I took another stroll down to the river, just to fix firmly in my mind what I was in for. I loved to watch and listen to the power of water, the roar of the rapids, the constant shuffling of pebbles on the river bed. I stood watching it for about fifteen minutes when a balsa raft came drifting by, over the rapids, a few spins and on its way. It was of the type that over-adventurous tourists sometimes make to try their luck on stretches of white water. Well, there was nobody on it now. I wondered if it had a story to tell.

The afternoon was spent sealing equipment into containers against water seepage.

By evening Señor Manga's eldest daughter came home from school and called into see how I was getting along. She was a bright and attractive girl of fifteen and wanted to know a little of my expedition. "My father tells me you are a rich man," she said. I was indeed rich by local standards but it was not an impression I liked to create. "No," I replied. "I just work hard and save hard. I don't drink, smoke or gamble." "How does this thing work?" she asked pointing at the kayak. So I sat in it and gave her a demonstration, pointing out the significance of my special paddle with its offset blades. She held the paddle and went through the motions herself. She caught on quickly.

I joined the family for supper and they had thought of a few more questions to ask me. To them I *must* be a rich man, flying all the way from Australia to spend months canoeing down a river. Did I have my own company in Australia? Or were some big companies sponsoring me for publicity purposes? No, I had no company or sponsors. It was just my own ambition. We discussed my work and the money I earned. Impressive sums to them, but they had little realisation of the cost of living in the western world.

It rained heavily for most of the night and following morning. I stayed indoors for the morning, continuing with the loading and balancing checks, weighing each item on my spring-balance. To reduce the bulk of things like oats, milk powder, washing powder and tea bags, I removed them from their original packets and compressed them into small plastic containers. I had to cut back further on clothes so I left behind a couple of T-shirts, a polo neck, a pair of gym shoes and, most reluctantly, my jeans. I had hoped to be able to use these whilst camping, as protection from the biting insects. Some of the fibreglass repair materials would also be abandoned although I was not too worried about this as I had allowed some in case of damage in transit and this had not been needed.

By afternoon the rain had stopped so I wandered down to the river. A few heavy logs coming down and levels had risen a bit. It did not look too serious here but what was the Pongo like? There were no roads beyond Quiteni, no way to observe the river beyond this point.

Strolling back, I spotted three men digging beside the river. I guessed they might be prospecting, but for what? "Is there gold here?" I asked. "*Si, señor,*" replied the eldest man happily. "*Oro aqui*" (gold here). He produced a tobacco tin filled with sand and fumbled his finger through it, indicating a few shiny flecks he believed to be gold.

By late evening, the cargo problem was as close to being solved as it would ever be. The kayak would be stern heavy no matter how I juggled the cargo. The rear cargo area was approximately double that of the forward and some of the heavier and larger items like the repair kit could only be accommodated here. I had discarded a few more items like a spare fibreglass roller, some extra hacksaw blades, and even four packs of freeze-dried food. Cargo weight was now thirty-three kilos, still heavier than desired, but margins were already too thin to risk further cut backs. The total weight of the cargo and kayak was fifty-six kilos while everything was dry. Once clothes and equipment got wet, this figure could change dramatically. My total equipment list (including items I would be wearing) is itemised in Appendix I.

After supper, I chatted with Señor Manga and watched him conduct his pharmacia business. A spare room in the house was used for this purpose. He seemed to be acting in the capacity of a doctor, giving advice or recommending some medicine. An Indian woman came. She had brought an interpreter with her to explain her problem. I could not help admiring her polite and placid approach – she was a lovely person.

I returned to my room and in the light of a candle wrote letters to my brother and the English journalist, Martin Trew. Just a few lines explaining where I was and that I would start my expedition on the morrow, 9th August.

Before turning in, I reminded myself of all the work and planning behind me and vowed 'never to give up'.

5 INTO THE RIVER

The big day arrived, Monday 9th August. The weather was fine and I joined Señor Manga and family and friends on the verandah for breakfast. I was asked to put my name in the family book and was wished well by all present. I got Señor Manga to write me a small note, stating the date and place of departure, just for record purposes. This he did and also got it witnessed.

"What time will you be off?" the family asked. "Before noon," I replied. Most of the cargo was packed into two nylon holdalls, ready to be carried down to the river. It was not wise to try carrying a fully loaded kayak. My documents and the bulk of my money, US$800 in cash, US$1100 in travellers' cheques, and 140,000 soles, were sealed in plastic bags and inserted into the pouches of my buoyancy vest. My gold finger rings were also inserted here as they were likely to attract the wrong kind of attention. I kept a smaller amount of money, approximately 20,000 soles, in my wallet for trading at the larger towns. No point in showing people where the bulk of my cash was kept. The wallet was sealed in a plastic bag and kept in the pocket of my khaki shorts.

Señor Manga and his friend carried the kayak shoulder high through the village while I carried the holdalls of cargo. By the time we reached the river most of the village had fallen in behind us − it was almost like a parade. I took some movie film of the crowd and they in turn took some of me. Somehow they managed to operate the camera upside down.

The cargo was neatly packed into the hatches, the spare paddle and poncho strapped to the fore deck, the camper mat to the stern. These three items were the only deck cargo. There were many questions from the villagers, mainly concerning my gadgets and equipment, and I gave a quick demonstration where possible. Most of my equipment was rather strange to them. I zipped my bright yellow buoyancy vest over my T-shirt and secured my wrist bands. Now I was ready for action.

By 1100 I slid the kayak into the river. Yes, it was stern heavy and it showed, but there was nothing I could do about it now. I shook hands with Señor Manga and his family and climbed into the cockpit. It was nearly two months since I had done any canoeing and a little practice was needed to get the feel of things. I paddled back and forth in an eddy for a few minutes, just to reassure myself, waved farewell to the crowd and eyed the first rapid. This was it! It is now or never, all or nothing; with three years' work behind me, I was going to give it all I'd got.

I was worried as I approached the rapid. This was no lightweight, white-water kayak I was in. Would three years' planning end abruptly right here? I aimed for the 'V', the area of maximum flow and least obstruction. The kayak rides well although a little deeper than desired, finding little support in such bubbly aerated water. I get the first shock of cold water as it trickles over the top of my spray cover. I plough through the stoppers, the standing waves at the bottom of the rapid. That's one rapid down and Christ knows how many to go. The brief take-off worries are gone now. It's just the exhilarating challenge before me. Soon the next rapid appears and again we ride it well. "Good ol' kayak," I can't help but say. I pass four more rapids in the first hour, my confidence increasing with each success. It can handle a grade three well. Then a stretch of flat water, a moment to relax. Lush green vegetation rises up on either side of me, birds sing and a pretty blue butterfly flits around the kayak. It's a beautiful world and I'm glad I came.

Soon, I hear the roar of the next rapid and firm my grip on the paddle. There is a gravel bed to the left of this one, so I take the opportunity to pull off the river and make an inspection. It is a grade four with a huge whirlpool to the right and a large eddy to the left. The whirlpool is about twenty feet across and I watch a log get swallowed into its eye. I could portage this rapid but it would mean a couple of hours' work unloading and loading the kayak. "Give it a go, you can make it." Some sharp manoeuvring around the boulders and restricted passages staying just left of the mainstream whilst keeping a cautious eye on the whirlpool. A drenching as I bulldoze through the stoppers and then speed on downstream.

By 1600 I have done enough for my first day and pull up on a stony beach. It is not a good camp spot but I did not expect to find much better in this region. I pick a spot thirty yards from the river. There is dry sand here and, after moving some of the larger stones, I should be able to make camp. I find some straight poles and try banging them into the sand to make a bivouac. But the ground is too stony so, for extra support, I make piles of stones around the base of the poles.

To get the kayak up here it will have to be unloaded. To try and drag it over this beach will certainly lead to disaster. Off come the main hatches and out comes all my neatly packed gear. Once the boat is empty, I carry it across to the camp. Using two spare paddle shafts for supports and my plastic poncho as a cover, I make a crude bivvy. With my camper mat on the ground and a space blanket to cover me, I should get a reasonable night's sleep. Wood is no problem, plenty of dead stuff lying around to get the fire going. Next I put on my dry set of clothes. Apart from the navy blue shorts they're identical to the first set. It is amazing what a boost dry clothes and a fire give to morale. As night comes closer, I gather all my gear together and enough wood to last the night and fill my water containers, putting in one purification tablet for each litre. I wear the spare sheath knife and keep the flashlight handy. Now for the best part of camping – a cooked meal. It is sliced lamb and peas tonight from one of my freeze-dried packs. Sling the contents into the billy can, bring the water to boil and simmer for a few minutes. That's the style of cooking I like. Delicious. Now a cup of tea to wash it down. Paradise. I wonder what they're all doing at home. Another exciting day at work? To hell with the rat race. This is my world. This is how to live.

I wore my spray jacket and kept the fire high for warmth, it's cold at night at this altitude, about three thousand feet. It would have been good to have had those jeans covering my legs but not to worry. By midnight I curled up on the camper mat with the space blanket over me. With its reflective surface turned inwards, I felt warm enough and soon dozed off.

About an hour later, fine rain started and a few trickles of water were running on to me. I shuffled myself around a bit and dozed off again. By 0300 it was raining steadily, the bivvy sagged and finally collapsed. There was nothing I could do so I pulled the plastic space blanket over me as best I could and tried to sleep some more. By dawn it was raining hard. I was soaked through and shivering. The river had risen a bit and was now a murky brown colour with lots of logs and debris coming down. There was nothing to be cheerful about this morning and even my only toilet roll was soaked through. Come on, come on; keep your discipline. Wash, shave and get a fire going.

It continued to rain for most of the morning and I struggled to keep the fire going. I almost got breakfast cooked and then tripped over the billy can. Oh well. Wash the sand off the meat and forget about the peas. Things were not going well today. Most of the gear, wet or not, was loaded back into the containers and moved towards the river. The soggy toilet roll was dumped, as was the half-towel. It was soaking wet and not essential cargo anyway. A spare T-shirt would do for a towel. Finally, I carried the kayak to the river's edge. It felt heavy this morning but I guess it was just the lack of sleep and general discomfort I was in.

Fitting the cargo in presented the usual problems and being wet and miserable did not help one to be neat and tidy. A wet pair of underpants could not find a place, so on to the fire they went. Two pairs would do for the trip.

All ready and set to go when seemingly from nowhere, a pair of Indians arrived on the scene, wearing what could be loosely described as western clothes. They were about mid to late teens and looked like brother and sister. Slowly and cautiously they approached the kayak, speaking quietly to each other as they moved. They came within fifteen feet and stopped. They were just curious. I wished them good day in Spanish and, understanding, they returned the greeting. For all my love of science and technology, I will for ever envy the smile of that girl. No business deals to clinch, no hidden meanings, just – hello, pleased to meet you. There was nothing in the plastic world to equal that.

By 1100 I was on my way. My clothes are wet but there is nothing I can do about that. Over the first rapid, over the second, both grade threes, and soon the aches and pains of wearing damp clothes are gone and it's back into the swing of things. By 1300 the sun shows its face and once more it's a

54

beautiful world. I seem to be passing through a wooded winding valley of lush green vegetation with high hills visible all around. I swirl past an Indian village neatly laid out with its thatched huts and a small Indian boy spots me. He bellows at the top of his lungs, "Hey, Gringo." It sounds so amusing as it echoes through the valley. The Indians were good. They often fish by the rapids and they knew the danger spots well. If I was off course as I approached a rapid, they would point the direction I should be for a safe passage. There was no fuss, no shouting, just a raised arm pointing the way. A time, a place, a set of circumstances, it couldn't mean anything else. They were very logical. I sometimes wondered why they bothered. I could not imagine the white man had done much for them.

There were very few rapids you could check in advance. They often occurred where the banks were steep or rocky and you could not get off the river to observe them. So I would just crane my neck, watch the flow and look for obstructions. My heart pounded at every one. If I was off course when I reached one, it was too late for correction: it was over the ledge into the boiling foam, the kayak spinning crazily; I would strike my paddle in for all I was worth, yelling and tightening every muscle. Then came the quiet stretches and a quick assessment of my performance: "well done", or "you were bloody lucky there". There were many hairy moments.

I watched the river winding down through the valley. A clear sensation of going downhill. I wondered how many more rapids before it bottoms out. I decided to take some movie film as I was travelling along. Logically not difficult on the flat-water stretches but a very precarious business in white water.

I hung the plastic movie camera around my neck with a piece of nylon rope and when conditions were fair I'd film with one hand whilst holding the paddle with the other. I tried to get as close to rapids as I could before having to drop the camera and get with the action. Reasonably safe on grades two and three, but if I had my doubts I wouldn't risk it. I tried running the camera tied to the side of my head and almost lost it over-board.

By 1600 I had had enough and got off the river. A small sand patch – this would do fine. I would make a better camp this time as I did not need a repeat of last night. I used my paddle to fashion the sleeping area out of the bank and found some poles to use as framework for a shelter. Elastic bands and tie wraps held the poles together and then I laid the plastic poncho over the top.

A couple of Indians came over in a canoe to see what I was up to. I told them I would just be stopping for the night and then on to Atalaya. They both started grinning, pointed down river and said in Spanish, "The Pongo Mainiqui is down there." "How far?" I asked. "About one hour," they replied. Kilometres or miles did not exist in their world, only the time it took to get somewhere by boat: an hour, a day, many days.

They asked if I had any nylon fishing line. I was rather expecting this question and asked how much they needed. One of them pointed out a distance along the bank – about twenty metres of line. "Can you get me some eggs tomorrow?" I asked. "Yes, and some fruit," they replied. I cut the twenty metres of line and bid them farewell.

The shelter looked sturdy enough, so I got a fire going and hung all my wet clothes out to dry. I did not have any dry clothes to put on so I kept the fire high and stayed close to it for warmth. With the wall of the camp behind me and no winds blowing it was tolerable. There was a footpath near the camp so I guessed somebody lived nearby. However, I was not feeling energetic enough to go and find out; in fact I was finding it hard to stay awake.

All the clothes were steaming. They should be dry in an hour or two. I put the billy can on and made supper: sliced beef and beans – what a fantastic cook I was! Five minutes and it was all done. By 2200 I was struggling to keep my eyes open. The clothes were still a bit soggy, I longed for a completely dry set to sleep in. I was just nodding off when two Indians walked past my camp carrying a sack on their shoulders. Pointing at the fire, one remarked, "*Pescado esta noche*" (fish tonight) and then proceeded further down the bank. I put some damp clothes on and tried to figure out what they meant. They stopped about thirty yards downstream and appeared to be poking about in the shallows. There were a few loud splashes, some excited talking and then I realised that they were using a net with weights around its perimeter, casting it into the river and pulling it in. Half an hour later, they were back and their sack was bulging. "How many kilos?" I asked. They each lifted it in turn and then handed it to me. "Thirty kilos?" suggested one man. "That's possible," I said. "Thirty kilos not bad for thirty minutes' fishing." A couple of the smaller fish were placed on the fire and the men sat down. Wearing remnants of western clothes they did not look like full Indians but mestizos and Spanish was spoken by both, so we were able to have a little discussion by the camp fire. They asked what I was doing there. "An expedition," I replied. "On my way to Atalaya and Pucallpa." "Are you looking for gold?" one asked. "No," I replied. "Is there gold here?" The answer was vague. The next question surprised me as they asked if I had an electronic metal detector in the kayak. "No," I replied, explaining that I was just travelling and doing some studies on the river. I felt it necessary to distract their thoughts away from the idea that I was in any way connected with gold prospecting. To tell them I was out to set a world canoeing record would make no sense to these people. To say I was doing a study of some kind and to indicate with my hand I was writing was more plausible. In essence this was true anyway.

They seemed to trust me more now and were having a little discussion amongst themselves as to whether or not they should show me something. Finally, one produced a carefully wrapped piece of paper and opened it. A few grams of gold flakes. Both were giggling. "Gold," said one. "Here?" I asked. "Yes, from here." "How much would that be worth?" one asked. I told him the international price of gold but I had no idea how much would be paid for it in Lima.

They asked me more about metal detectors and if they were any good. I mentioned their fine points and also their limitations. I had owned one of the finest models available as I had been prospecting for gold in Australia and knew they were far from foolproof. There is no detector in the world that can positively tell you that there's gold in the ground. The better ones can discriminate between ferrous and non-ferrous metals but not much more than that. Someone had been spinning these guys a good tale for their impression was that detectors were magical devices that could sniff out gold everywhere and anywhere. Soon I became extremely drowsy so I thanked the men for the fish, we bid each other good night, and within minutes I was fast asleep.

At the crack of dawn on 11th August, the two Indians were back with four eggs and a pile of mixed fruit, including bananas, oranges and something similar to the delicious Asian starfruit. They did not hang around as there was probably fishing to be done; after listening to my polite "Thank you", they were on their way.

Well, it was Pongo day today. The river had risen another foot and a half, and, needless to say, I had the butterflies. The weather was fine, so I hung everything out for a proper drying and then got breakfast under way.

After a shave and a good wash in the river, I was fit for anything. At 0700 a man stopped by in his canoe. He was not full-blooded Indian and he was not on a fishing trip for in the bottom of his boat was a large conical-shaped wooden plate that looked like a China-man's hat, a wooden version of a gold pan. My kayak fascinated him and he asked me about the gadgets on it. The pump intrigued him most of all; it seemed real space-age stuff to the Indians who carried a wooden bowl in their canoes for bailing purposes. He lived near by and obviously knew the area well. I pointed at the first rapid and asked how many more there were before the Pongo. He got a stick and made a map of the river in the sand. He drew lines across it which represented the rapids. "This one's nothing," he would say, "and this one's big," and "this one's very big." I pointed at the first rapid and asked where the best place was to pass; "that side, or this?" "Centre," he said. "And how about these?" I asked, pointing at the map. He ran his finger through the sand, saying, "This one, this side; this one, this side. And, caution here – that's the big one." I drew the map on a loose leaf from my notebook and studied it. I wanted that map printed on my brain.

Next we discussed the gold and he gave me a demonstration with his gold pan. I took some movie film of him and then he moved on to his prospecting ground which was about a quarter of a mile downstream.

About ten o'clock I stopped for tea and thought over the trip so far. The good performances and the near misses. I analysed each situation; why I had done well at this point, and how I nearly came a cropper at the next. What could have been done to avoid that. I would visualise the situation in my mind, a type of action-replay, carefully analysing my performance and noting the corrective action that must be taken.

By late morning, the sun was scorching. A cup of coffee at midday and the butterflies were still with me. It would be all right once the action started. It always was. I looped a length of shock cord around the outside of my buoyancy vest, passing it under my armpits; this in turn would be hooked on to the deck line of my kayak. Strictly against the safety rules, but so was everything else I was doing. I could not afford to be separated from my kayak and equipment here.

The first rapid was straightforward, a grade two; the second, between grade two and three, presented a few problems – the safest passage did not conform with my friend's explanation; in fact it was quite the opposite. It was not too difficult to handle, but I decided to forget about the map and play it by sight. I do not think I have been lied to, but I believe what happened was that he had only marked the rapids he could remember, or had not bothered to mention the minor ones. In fact, I think the latter case was more likely. It was now impossible to know which rapids he considered significant and which he did not. The next rapid I reached gave the appearance of a weir, just an unbroken line visible on the top of it. I scanned from side to side, trying to find the optimum position but, too late, I found myself at the edge of a four-foot ledge. With a loud scraping and graunching sound, the kayak slid over the top, nose-dived in to the water below and came to an abrupt stop. The action of the weir was now dragging me back up against the waterfall, so I dug the paddle in like I was going for Olympic gold: "Go, go, go." Slowly I moved clear of the weir's clutches and finally beyond its reach. Paddle going full bore, I shot downstream, the water running with me at over ten knots, and a sensation like a snapped piece of elastic, catapulting me off.

A few minutes' recuperation and soon the next one is in sight. The waters boiling again, jetting high into the air as it crashes into and over the boulders that impede its flow, it would take one hit to reduce the kayak to splinters.

At 100 yards the right side looks the best passage, the water speeds as it funnels into the rapid. At fifty yards it's a different picture – back to the left. Seconds are ticking by – where shall I take it? Luck's in! There's "old honest Indian" sitting on a rock fishing, almost expressionless with his brown smock and red painted face, but there is the sign I am looking for – a raised arm pointing to a spot about two-thirds across the river. "Get over," the arm motions, "get over." The rapids roar and soon I am in the middle of the mainstream going for all I'm worth. It's a grade four with boils, swirls and boulders everywhere. Go left, hard right then straighten up, slap the paddle down for support – "Go, go, go" and we are through. Thank God those Indians never lied.

The river opens up and slows a little here with some gently tapered pebble beaches. The sun's intensity increases and there's no mistaking what's in front of me, those huge rocky cliffs where the river is funnelled through. I was on the last stretch of flat water before the Pongo.

I back-paddled for a while and mentally prepared myself for it. Once in there, there is no turning back. Three miles of white water and, if I make a mistake, there is little chance of rescue. I look the kayak over for the last time; hatches secure, spare paddle in place, spray cover secure and in I go. How those words echoed in my ears as I approached the entrance – "It can be nothing or a death trap."

Sheer granite cliffs block out the sunlight, the roar of the rapid fills my ears. I look for the clearest channel and give it all I've got. The kayak gets tossed and turned. I feel it start to go over and dig my paddle in for all I'm worth. "Move, you son of a bitch, move," cursing both myself and the kayak. My watch strap snaps and it slides down my arm. I grab it with my teeth and keep with the action. I make it through the first one, and then the second, and then the third. "Good ol' kayak; good ol' kayak. We're going to make it." I am very close to my kayak now. It is my life support system and I cannot survive without it. A small stretch of flat water, a few moments' rest to admire the beauty of the place. Crystal-clear water cascades from above. It is a magnificent sight. I move towards the cliff face to try to catch a solitary trickle of water to drink from above but soon a swirl and the kayak starts to spin. How could anything be so beautiful and yet so treacherous? I thrust the paddle in to correct. This is no place to relax. Push on, push on. Energy is getting burnt up at a high rate. The consequences of a mistake need not be spoken. I see the end of the Pongo now, The Gateway, and light is increasing as it opens to the great expanses beyond. A couple more rapids, a few more hairy moments and I am through.

I carry on for a while until I find a quiet spot to unwind and take stock of the situation. No damage to the kayak, no cargo lost, and I am still in one piece. As I look back to the Pongo I feel relieved and happy. It is a magnificent place, but respect it you must.

It was too early to make camp yet, so I gently paddled on. Only grade two rapids to contend with here, and the banks rose less steeply. This was the start of the great Amazon Basin. I could see for several miles now and felt less confined. The vegetation was everything you would expect the Amazon to be; an infinite variety of trees and rich, green foliage. It was quiet and peaceful. I could relax for I felt I was through my first major obstacle.

6 REMOTE AREAS

The area I was now entering was remote and almost totally outside the money economy. In the rainy season, when the river is in flood, its velocity is so great that it tears down its banks and thunders on its way filled with huge trees and tangled debris: it is too dangerous for boats to venture up. Now in the dry season, the river is low, exposing shifting pebbly banks and sandy shoals: cargo vessels seldom visit for fear of running aground.

By evening I found a small sand patch to the side of one of the islands, close to the water and easy to drag my kayak up on to. There were a few pieces of driftwood around so I started to gather them. Across the river was a solitary hut, the first I had seen since passing the Pongo. A young boy at the water's edge was looking in my direction. I waved but he never responded. I found some bamboo poles and was about to start erecting camp when a balsa raft appeared on the scene. A man dressed in a pair of shorts that looked as if they had been manufactured from the remnants of about a dozen other pairs, pulled up on to the bank. He looked at the kayak and then at me, and pointing his fingers to his mouth, asked if I wanted to eat. I pointed to the camp spot and said I would eat here. Pointing in the direction of the hut, he said, "No. Eat there." Why not? I thought. I had not unpacked the kayak and this would be a good opportunity to meet the locals.

Facing the kayak upstream, I kept the nose into the flow and cautiously ferry-glided across without letting the boat come side-on to the current which was strong here. The balsa raft was taken upstream to a point at the base of the last rapid. With considerable skill and experience, it was manoeuvred through the eddies and turbulence, across to the far bank and allowed to race downstream to the hut.

The young boy was still standing by the river, but he never spoke and did not seem happy. There were in fact two huts. One was a combined kitchen and chicken coop; the other was for sleeping. There were five people altogether; two men, one in his early twenties and the other about thirty; one woman about twenty-five, and also two children. The children were both boys, one about twelve and the other perhaps two. There appeared to have been a tragedy somewhere. The twelve-year-old boy was without mother and I think that accounted for his sorrow. He rarely smiled and hardly ever spoke.

After meeting everybody, I pulled the kayak out of the water and asked the elder man if it would be safe there. He assured me it would. It was a stupid question as there was nobody else around to take it.

The huts were very basic; bamboo poles for the walls and an open space for the door, a thatched roof and a mud floor. A crude bench and table had been erected in one corner of the kitchen and a mud fireplace opposite. A fifty-kilo sack of salt hung above the fireplace to keep dry. It seemed to have been there for some time as the outside was heavily sooted. Outside the kitchen was a hollowed-out tree-trunk, used for pounding the rice, and an abundance of fish lying on slats to dry. The lady of the house later told me it was kept in salt for three days and then put in the sun to dry. It was obviously more fish than they would ever need, so a bit of bartering or trading was going on.

We sat down to a supper of rice and heavily salted fish, and soon hints about nylon fishing line were being dropped. Did I have any in my kayak? "Yes," I said, and promised to give them some in the morning. Their language was the South American dialect of Spanish and not too difficult to understand. Would they like some coffee, I asked? Smiles all round and yes, they would. I produced Nescafé and saccharine tablets and we all had an enjoyable drink.

Nylon fishing line was unbelievably scarce. The men told me it would cost around a thousand soles for twenty metres. It was superior to any lines they could produce locally and was in heavy demand. The home-made oil lamp started to flicker and soon we were all starting to think about bed. The lady of the house had produced a sheepskin rug for me to lie on. "Won't you be cold?" one of the men asked. "No," I replied, producing my space blanket. "This will keep me warm." Not understanding how a thin plastic sheet could do that, I doubt if they believed me for one minute. The family retired to their hammocks in the second hut and I curled up comfortably on the kitchen floor, using my buoyancy vest as a pillow.

The chickens and pigs gave me an early call, right at the crack of dawn, scrounging around before the family was up. Shortly after, the woman came in and started chopping up wood for the fire. I took a stroll down to the river to see ol' kayak. Yes, she was still there waiting for orders! I got washed and cleaned up, and returned to the hut for breakfast. Rice and salted fish again, but this time some yuca, a potato-like root, thrown in. A mug of black tea to wash it down. Paradise! I was fit for anything.

I got the fishing line and hooks from my kayak and also my camera. As soon as Mum saw the camera, she picked up her son and disappeared from the scene. She was not afraid of cameras; she just wanted to tidy up a bit. We measured off twenty metres of fishing line and I gave it to the men, together with a few hooks. Soon, mother and son were back and both were dressed in their best, bright woollen jumpers probably made by herself. She adored that child – nothing was too good for him. Junior posed well and Mum was delighted. The only sad point was that she would never see the photographs. There was no address and no postal service in this part of the world.

I took my gear down to the kayak and started to load up. The eldest boy followed me down and discreetly asked for fishing line and hooks for himself. He wanted his independence from the others, so I gave him some. The rest of the group then appeared to watch me make final preparations. Most interesting to watch was the youngest child's relaxed reaction to the environment: he was so at peace with the world. A bird would give its morning chorus from a nearby tree and gently, he turned his head in its direction to absorb it all. There were no sharp movements, just a total acceptance that this was his world.

There were a few jokes about gringo's equipment and one of the men asked why I always wore the buoyancy vest. I told him it was warm and comfortable. I could not tell him I had over $2000 stuffed away in it. I felt like asking him why he always wore a sack over his head, as I had never seen him take it off since I had been there. However, I guessed he might have a problem so I decided to hold my tongue.

The night had been too damp to dry any clothes, so I had to pack them wet. I thanked the lady of the house for the food and gave her 1000 soles, hoping she could make use of it. She rushed back to the hut and got me another helping of fish and yuca to take with me. I was most grateful. So by 0900 it was farewells and thank yous all round, and I was on my way.

It is a sparsely populated area and rather pleasant to canoe through, dense trees or cane grass grown right down to the banks. Occasionally the river narrowed and speeded up a bit and then it opened into great wide areas where the gradient was less and the river slowed, dropping off mounds of stones. You could hear the pebbles shifting on the river bed, every day wearing thinner and moving further downstream.

I was just approaching a rapid, when I spotted my first crocodile. He was about six feet long and, according to what I have read and been told, crocs up to that size usually do not attack you. I was hoping this crocodile possessed the same information. Slowly but deliberately, it slid down the bank and made its way out to midstream, its mean, beady eyes clearly visible above the surface. The rapid in front of me was only grade two, but I could not help thinking of the consequences of screwing up and capsizing. You could not outrun a croc and you certainly could not outswim one. As I came parallel with it, it abruptly turned and dived. I believed I was safe now but couldn't be sure. Perhaps he was manoeuvring under the kayak and would attempt to capsize me. A burst of speed might leave him behind but I still gave the occasional glance over my shoulder.

By midday, I found a crystal-clear stream adjoining the main river and could not resist a little splash around. It is hard to explain what something like that means to you when you have been sweating under the blazing sun for hours. It is like looking at a river of sweet wine. I filled my water bottle, added a purification tablet, and took a break. This was a good spot for a meal, so I got out the fish and yuca and had a delicious lunch. I paddled back to the main river, scanning the tree-line above for smoke. The main river narrowed here and rocky cliffs rose on either side. I expected an Indian camp for it was an ideal site, the junction of two rivers, with a high look-out place. It was their dug-out canoes tied to the base of a cliff which gave them away. A small group of them was wandering up a track at the side of a cliff, making for a clearing at the top. I guessed they might have some fruit to trade, so I called out to them. They looked back for a moment and then increased their speed up to the camp. A different, much larger group now came to the edge of the clearing and peered down; I waved but they were not sure what to make of me. Eventually a few people wandered back down the track, until they were within ten yards of me. In halting Spanish I asked, "Do you have bananas here?" They just shook their heads, either not understanding or not wanting to trade. They were Machiguenga Indians. Their dress was simple; just a reddish-brown handwoven smock, something like a poncho hanging straight from the shoulders. They never showed any hostility but I doubt if they wanted any close relationships with the outside world. An abundance of food and a contented way of life. What could we offer them? I took some movies and paddled on.

There were very few sandy patches or beaches amongst the stony islands I passed, so it looked as if I would have a fair amount of work to do in organising camp tonight. It did not get dark till 1800 but I needed a couple of hours to get camp organised so at 1600 I pulled off the river on to a stony beach. There was a small sand patch twenty yards higher up on the island, but a lot of large rocks would have to be moved before I could get the kayak up there. I set to with a will, rolling boulders and big stones clear until I had cleared a path way. It was hard work after a day's canoeing but it had to be done before I could drag the kayak up to the campsite. There were smears of white gel-coat left on the smaller stones and gravel it had passed over, and I gave thought to how many times I could do that before wearing a hole in the bottom.

Nearby were the remains of an abandoned shelter left by the Indians. I had seen them before, just a simple bamboo lean-to to get shade from the sun while they cut and clean their fish. I removed the poles and set about building my own camp. My skills were improving although my efforts could not be classified as stormproof but they were sturdy enough to take a reasonable amount of wind and rain. Six or seven bamboo poles were enough for the framework and the cover was invariably my plastic poncho.

High on the priority list before darkness fell, was wood-gathering because it was hopeless walking around in the dark, tripping over rocks looking for sticks and branches. I managed to get all chores done by dusk and soon had a good feed of potato casserole, followed by a cup of tea. By 2000 I was ready for bed. I estimated that I had travelled thirty-five miles that day but was unsure of my exact location as there were no significant landmarks in this part of the country and the maps I had were far from adequate. However, previous experience with the kayak told me that a steady paddling rate would average five knots. To this I would add the average current velocity for the day and have a reasonable idea where I was. The average current here was one and a half knots. After putting another couple of logs on the fire, I crawled into my shelter and fell asleep.

Friday the thirteenth was going to be fine, the skies were clear and I was not superstitious. I hung my clothes out to dry and stoked the fire up. There were extra footprints around the camp which were certainly not mine – they were the real wide foot of the Indian. I checked my gear and nothing was missing; my throat had not been cut nor my equipment stolen, so there was nothing to fear from such people.

It was porridge for breakfast this morning; first I mixed two or three large tablespoons of dry oats with milk powder and sugar, then added this to the boiling water, stirring for a couple of minutes while it simmered. Easy to prepare and tastes good, that's how I like things! Soon the sun was intense so I got the solar panel out to recharge my torch batteries. Next I set the camera up on a rock, adjusted the timer and took a couple of shots of myself around the camp fire. With all these modern gadgets, there was nothing a one-man expedition could not achieve.

At 1000 I made tea, took my anti-malarial Maloprin tablet and brought my log up to date. I was reasonably happy about everything with the exception of the daily loading and unloading of my kayak. It was a tiring job and was taking too much time. I was in no hurry but the time could be better spent, visiting Indian villages or doing some photography. So, this would be my task for the next week: reduce turn-around time.

The batteries got about three and a half hours' charge and that would top them up. The charger put out seventy miliamps at maximum sunlight and that was enough for my requirements. Just a couple of hours each day while I was fixing breakfast and drying clothes was all that would be needed.

By midday, yesterday's wet T-shirt and shorts were dry, my fresh-water container was full and it was time to go. The fresh-water container had proved to be a good idea: firmly wedged beside the seat so it would not fall out if I capsized, I could get a mouthful whenever I needed it through a two-foot long, quarter-inch-bore plastic tube. This was particularly important on days of clear blue skies and scorching sun when the temperature reached into the eighties F, and the air was still rarefied.

I was still in the department of Cuzco, and still on the Urubamba river flowing north, but the altitude steadily decreased down the Andean foothills. There was almost no white water now and for the most part the river was smooth, if fast flowing. There was a steady current to urge me along and I paddled with an easy practised action. I was getting into my stride and could keep up a good pace for hours on end. Good progress could be made by reading water and making use of maximum flow areas. If the sun became too intense I would reduce my paddling rate and try to get shadow from the tree-lined banks.

I passed an Indian in his dugout and half a mile further on two Indian boys paddling a balsa raft, with a live chicken for cargo. This was almost certainly a father and his two sons, off to do some trading further downstream. I took some movie of them but they remained expressionless. As long as I was no threat to them, I was merely tolerated. By mid-afternoon I had a sudden urge for a coffee and pulled off the river. The sand was burning my feet and I had to stand in the river while the billy boiled. A short while later, the balsa raft passed me again and then came father in his dugout. He pulled up on to a beach about fifty yards from me and made his way through a section of dense cane grass. He was carrying a bow and arrows to do some hunting.

By 1600 I was close to Camisea and the Indian settlements

were becoming larger and more numerous. Some rugged-looking youths pulled alongside my kayak, and kept pace with me. For young fellows, they certainly had an abundance of scars on their faces and I could not help wondering how they had got them. The kayak intrigued them and they could not understand how it worked at all. They kept pace with me for about half a mile and then broke off.

By 1630 I was at Camisea. Here, the river Camisea forms a junction with the Urubamba and, predictably, there were Indian settlements, very large ones. I tied the kayak up and scaled the bank. A man who I took to be the head of the settlement came forward to see what I wanted. "Do you have bananas?" I asked. "Yes. How many?" I showed him a bunch of ten. "Do you want nylon fishing line?" "Yes," he said with no hesitation and, curling his finger, he said, "Some hooks, too." He certainly knew how to bargain which wasn't surprising since a settlement of this size would almost certainly be trading fish or surplus crops for such items as machetes or sugar with the larger towns of Shepahua or Atalaya further down the river. I asked permission to film the camp and this was granted. A youth of about sixteen kept looking down at the kayak and sniggering. His father talked to him sternly, but he had a hard time containing himself. By the time I left, he was ready to split his sides. I guess the kayak did look a little strange to him, especially now that I had a pair of flip-flops secured to the deck. Perhaps he thought I walked on water.

There was about half an hour left before dark so I got under way. Two miles further downstream I found a stony island with a small sand patch on it. Quickly I gathered a pile of firewood and moved the larger stones out of the way so I could drag the kayak up. Then it occurred to me that it would save a lot of wear and tear on the bottom of the kayak if I were to use a few large-diameter bamboo poles which were lying on the beach as rollers. I put one underneath, pulled the kayak up a few feet, put another roller under and pulled it up a bit more. Ten minutes of this and the boat was at my camp site. Now everything was in position, I got a nasty shock. There were some crocodile footprints at the edge of the river. I tried to work out its size and estimated it to be about four feet. If I was right, it should be no problem, but I am no expert on crocodiles' footprints. The island was about half a mile long and a quarter of a mile wide, low-lying and ninety per cent large stones. In the last light of day, I scanned in all directions and couldn't spot anything; if it was still around, then it had camouflaged itself very well. I fashioned myself a nice stout club from a piece of hard wood. Not the best defence in the world, but if the croc was not too big, then a stiff clout across his nose should deter him. Just in case of a night-time visit, I erected poles around the camp with nylon rope tied between them and then balanced stones and cooking utensils on top. If anything tripped over the rope, there should be enough clatter to wake me up. I built the fire up high and, keeping a constant watch over my shoulder, began to cook.

There was an occasional splash in the river, but it was not wise to let my imagination run away with me: it could be just a large fish. I sat by the fire eating and occasionally scanned the area with my flash light. The large logs made me jump a little, as the light scanned past them. By 2100 I felt pretty safe and gave the area a last search with my flashlight. Nothing moved, nothing in sight, so I turned in for the night.

I awoke just after dawn. The fire was still smouldering and a mist covered the river. An Indian was standing by me: better than a crocodile. I wished him the time of day and he returned the compliment. I told him that I was heading for Atalaya and his face brightened. He squatted down by the fire and did not seem to be in a hurry to go anywhere. His dugout canoe was pulled on to the beach, so I strolled over to check it out. Gouged out of a single tree-trunk, it was well made and very solid, a skill passed down from generation to generation. The head of the single-bladed paddle gave the appearance of the Ace of Spades, and like the canoe, it was heavy and rugged, but not particularly efficient, compared to the streamlined models of today. I handed him my all-fibreglass paddle and the weight surprised him. "*No peso,*" he said. (No weight.) I gave him twenty metres of fishing line as I guessed that was what he was here for. Pointing to the dugout, he asked me if I wanted some fish. "No," I replied, pointing to a pack of freeze-dried food. "I have food here." Soon he was off and I was enjoying a breakfast of sliced lamb and peas. After taking a photo of the camp, I went down to have another look at the crocodile prints. A croc definitely had been here despite the number of uncomfortable stones to walk over or lie on: he was probably just passing through.

By 1000 the mist had gone and the sun was intense. This was when time would start getting wasted because I would be sweating heavily and simple jobs would be tiring and would take too long to perform. Bending over to pack the kayak with the sun beating on your back was a sure way to wear you down. By 1030 I was on my way. Lots of flat water, just the occasional rapid. The sun was really giving me a hard time. Not only was I getting the effects of its direct rays, but I was also getting its reflections from the mirror surface of the river. Depending on the angle of the sun, you can get up to a hundred-per-cent increase of intensity like this. I had my bush hat on, sunglasses and also a long sleeved cotton polo neck shirt. This protected my neck, arms and head, but there was not much I could do about my face. The block-out cream helped, but sweating a lot tended rapidly to reduce its effectiveness. The worst part was my lips which were cracked and dry. Reluctantly, I decided it would be better to grow a beard. I had been shaving regularly up to this point and believe it increases discipline and morale, essential for a trip like this.

Not much activity in the areas I was passing, just the occasional Indian fishing from his canoe. If I waved, they usually waved back. They remained quite expressionless. I guessed it was difficult for a people who were only concerned with living from day to day to understand the logic of an expedition like mine. About once an hour, I would take a few sips from the water bottle and occasionally eat a banana. By 1600 I estimated I had covered thirty miles and had been paddling in the heat for over five hours so I started to look for a camp site. By 1630 I spotted a beach just below a rapid. The rapid was a grade two with a few nastily positioned tree-trunks across it, a trap to the unwary. Once over, I swung the kayak round and up on to the beach. There was plenty of driftwood, a few stones and no croc prints.

Scenery was changing a bit now; large rocks and pebbles gradually giving way to sandy beaches. The river banks were getting more uniform, just a few feet above the river and adorned with trees or tall plumed cane grass. An occasional bluff would have a clearing for an Indian camp. There appeared to be a deserted hacienda on the opposite bank of the river and it rather intrigued me. With my binoculars, I could see cattle roaming around and a few Indians. It seemed out of place here and had possibly been abandoned.

The weather was much warmer now and being wet for a long period of time was more tolerable. Even the nights were warmer. The average daytime temperature in the Amazon Basin is between 27° and 32°C (80° and 90°F) and during the warmest months, from September to November, it seldom drops below 21°C (70°F) at night. The only disadvantage was the warmer weather brought the mosquitos. They were not a serious problem at this stage and smoke from the camp fire usually deterred them. The nasty part was getting sharply bitten on the back of the hand as you were removing a boiling billy from the fire. Camps were easy to erect in the sand and, soon after supper, I was into bed and sound asleep.

The next day, 15th August, was fine. It did not seem to rain much in this area but I was feeling a few aches and pains, mainly due to wearing damp or wet clothes for too long.

Things got organised a bit more quickly today and I was under way by 0830. Indian camps were becoming larger again and, judging by the assortment of pots and pans, they must be doing a fair amount of trading. There was a small mestizo town, Shepahua, about a day's canoeing downstream from here and that was probably where the trading was done. My supply of bananas had run out so today's task was to get some more. The first village I stopped at had none to spare. It was a fairly large village with a population of about 200 people and innumerable vociferous yapping dogs. Rather than see me go empty handed, a woman gave me three dried fish. I thanked her and gave her 500 soles. She looked at the note for a moment, as if saying, "Well, what am I supposed to do with this?" She was still holding it as I got into my kayak and paddled away. I guessed somebody in the village could make use of it. It was late afternoon before I finally got the bananas, a large bunch for twenty metres of nylon fishing line. With half strapped to the stern and half on the bow, I set off to find a camp site.

The further downstream I travelled, the better the camp sites were. The stones were getting smaller and the sandy beaches becoming more numerous. Driftwood was always in abundance. There was another abandoned shelter on the beach, so I took the poles to make my camp. I would have liked to have seen the Indians erect these shelters. They were simple but very effective devices: a framework, three or four bamboo poles, and a series of palm leaves wrapped over them. I doubt if they took more than an hour to erect and yet they were sturdy enough.

The usual routine now was supper around 1900 and bed at 2100. Sleep was no problem, especially if it was soft dry sand, not rocks, to lie on. Occasionally I awoke in the night, perhaps an animal nearby or a large insect moving around under the camper mat. More often than not, I slept right through to early morning; just before dawn was a typical time to wake.

Monday, 16th August was another fine day. Porridge for breakfast and a check of the maps. My estimated position was twenty miles from Shepahua and I should reach there by mid-afternoon. Hopefully, there would be a store there to get some tinned food and eggs. I still had plenty of freeze-dried food, but considered it wise to retain it for as long as possible.

It had been quite a while now since I had passed any significant rapids and I did not anticipate too many in front of me. So I connected the fin on to the kayak to improve the directional stability. By 0915 I was on my way and the effect of the fin was immediately noticeable, a straighter course and less yawing about. By 1130 I had passed Sancha and ran into some heavy rain. Visibility was close to zero, so I stopped canoeing. I did not see the sense of running into a log or other obstruction.

At 1345 I reached the frontier town of Shepahua, the border town between the departments of Cuzco and Loreto. It is here that the river Urubamba takes on the name of the Ucayali. The amount of building going on surprised me; heavy machinery everywhere and an oil refinery being constructed. Significant amounts of oil have been discovered in the Amazon Basin, which will be taken out by giant oil barges of exceptionally shallow draught.

The town proper lay a short distance up the Rio Shepahua; with two very basic *pensions*, each with its own restaurant, it was not dissimilar to Quiteni. In true Latin style, it was siesta time and the owners of the restaurants were fast asleep on the verandahs, so I had a browse round while the owners slept and realised that the restaurants were also the only stores in the village. The range of goods was exceedingly small and, considering the amount of construction going on here, I was astonished. A few tins of milk, soap, stale bread with ants crawling all over it and eggs. I woke one of the restaurant owners and bought six stale bread rolls, a tin of milk and three eggs. I would have liked more eggs but they looked as if they had been lying around as long as the bread. That cost me 1250 soles, much too dear but this far out in the jungle it was a seller's market. There were a few bunches of bananas hanging outside, almost certainly brought there by the Indians. He wanted 2000 soles a bunch, which again was rather steep. I knew I could do better than that downstream, so I paddled on.

Most of the construction was taking place on the Ucayali side of town, so I moved in close hoping to find a better store. There was a boat, probably up from Atalaya, unloading stores and provisions about half-way down the bank. I asked one of the construction workers if it was possible to buy any of the goods but he told me it was not, as it was company-supplied food for the construction workers. He did offer me a tin free, but I declined the offer and thanked him anyway.

It would not be long before I was in Atalaya and I could get all I wanted there, so I paddled on. Motor boats frequently passed me with groups of construction workers on board. A lot of the labour for the refinery must have been recruited locally from mestizos or Indians.

By 1600 I was looking for a camp site. There was an island visible about half a mile downstream and it seemed to be what I was looking for. As I passed the junction of a small river, a group of Indians spotted me. I waved and asked for bananas. A few minutes later the whole group came down to the water's edge, one bearing the fruit. "What do you want for the bananas?" I asked. He shrugged his shoulders, eyed the bunch, and said, "Five hundred." The bunch was about the same size I had been offered at Shepahua for 2000. They asked me where I was going and where I slept at nights. I told them my destination was Pucallpa and I slept on sand banks. "How about food?" they asked. "Food is here," I said, pointing to the hatches. "No problem at night?" they asked, without specifying from what. "No problems," I replied. They smiled and shook their heads. One of the men brought a water melon down and divided it up between us. It was delicious.

Time was pressing, so I waved farewell and was once more on my way. The island looked good and soon I had a camp organised. It was chilli con carne and stale bread for supper, followed by bananas and a cup of tea.

I'd been paddling for a week since I left Quiteni and it was time for an assessment. According to the experts, I should be dead by now but I was definitely alive and enjoying myself; apart from a few minor aches and pains, I was still in good shape. The dysentery problem had long since gone. It was only a question of hygiene: simple things like boiling the Amazon water for fifteen minutes or using purification tablets were all that was needed. People had been good, and right now I would sooner be here doing this than anything else in the world.

I was quite enjoying the evening, sitting by the fire and thinking over the trip. About 2100 I was about ready to turn in when a motorised canoe came close by the island and spotted me. The engine was cut and the boat drifted in. One of the men aboard folded back a plastic sheet showing me his cargo – a great stack of whisky bottles. I told him that I was not interested, so they started the motor again and took off. They were boot-legging for sure; with the construction going on here, there would certainly be a market for it. I doubt whether they cared much where or who they sold the stuff to. Indian villages would be fair game, bringing to an end a peaceful way of life.

It rained for most of the night, but the bivvy held and I slept well. The morning was overcast but this was no problem; a cloudy day made canoeing easier. I was under way by 0830 and making good progress. The river opened out into some wide shallow areas, forming lots of islands as the river slowed. Great piles of trees that had been uprooted and dragged downstream, during the last flood, had dropped off here. Islands were piled high with them. It was like a graveyard of trees.

It was difficult to pick the best channel through because I

could not tell which side the final exit would be and the river was wide here. I just zig-zagged through the islands, trying to spot the best flow rates. There were none worth mentioning. It was just glassy-calm and silent. Frequently I would find myself in the shallows between two islands. My kayak got worn a bit thinner as she scraped over the stones.

By 1500 I guessed I was coming up to the police check point of Colonia Penal del Sepa which I had been warned about. The river opened out once more with a couple of islands to get round. The far left-hand stream seemed to have the best flow, so I followed it down. Two men in a motorised canoe seemed to be trying to advise me against it, pointing to the far side of the river. I was well into the stream by now, so it was a bit late to change. It was soon apparent why they were trying to warn me, for the river Sepa joins the Ucayali here and it was a far-from-gentle meeting. The water began to boil and whirls formed. I tried to edge towards the islands in midstream but was hindered by logs and debris being churned round and round in the turbulence. Poor frail ol' kayak skidding about amongst all those baulks of timber. Keep that paddle digging in; move, you bugger, move. The edge of the turbulence catches me and there goes my deck cargo of bananas. I am running with the mainstream at last and life looks better; I skim along to the bottom of the cliff face and on to the edge of a bank.

The check point was strategically placed on top of the cliff giving them a panoramic view of the river. Nobody got past without their knowing. I made my way up to a small hut where a couple of police officers were waiting. We shook hands and they wished me the time of day. They were very smartly dressed and very correct in attitude. I produced my passport and letters of introduction. "Did you come through the Pongo with that thing?" the corporal asked. "Yes," I replied, "no problems." With my limited knowledge of language, it would have been difficult to explain what problems I did have. The corporal raised his eyebrows; the sergeant looked more scep-tical. After entering my particulars into the log, the corporal accompanied me back down to my kayak. I showed him all the gadgets and where I kept my supplies. We shook hands again and he wished me *bon voyage*. "There's another control point about a mile downriver," he said, pointing in its direction. "And caution at Atalaya, the Rio Tambo will give you problems."

This second control point was hard to find, as it was just a hut on the opposite bank, concealed by the jungle and probably more concerned about upstream traffic. I had thoughts about giving it a miss altogether, but it was not wise to upset anybody. After wading through a mudbank, I made my way up the stairs to find the officer in charge fast asleep on his bed and a miserable-looking accomplice polishing his shoes on the verandah.

Colonia Penal del Sepa was a prison camp where the bad boys from Lima were sent. There was a fully loaded revolver lying on the table so I presumed that the accomplice must have been a trustee prisoner; he proceeded to wake his boss up and tell him there was a gringo here. I handed over all my documents again and the officer sent his trustee down to check my kayak. With all the delicate equipment I had, I thought it better to go with him. "One moment," I said, "I'll come." "He's all right; he's my friend," said the officer. "My equipment's very delicate," I said, but the officer did not seem fully awake. Just as expected, the trustee sat on the rear deck while he tried to get the hatches open. I rushed down, calling out to him, "It's very delicate, it's glass fibre." The officer followed me down and asked to see the cargo. I opened the hatches and he kept peering in, saying, "What's in that one? Open this one. What's this for?" It was getting close to dark now and I still had to find a camping spot. The mosquitos were biting my legs and how much more of the kayak I had to unload, I had no idea. After getting my cameras out, the officer seemed to have a better idea what I was up to. "Ah," he said, "you're on an expedition." "Yes," I replied. "Are you writing about it?" "Oh yes," I told him. "How about a photo of us with the kayak?" "Certainly," I answered, knowing that this would be the ticket out of here. I took the photo, shook hands and was on my way again.

Less than half an hour to go before dark and no camping spots in sight, just some wide, shallow areas, but no suitable beaches. The best I could find was a muddy bank on the edge of a settlement. There was no one in sight but I could hear a dog barking. It was pointless to try and wash, as I had to wade out through the mud to reach the river and back through it again to reach the camp.

I lit a fire to give me light to make the camp and then got the supper organised. It was a most uncomfortable evening. I felt dirty, grotty and irritable. After supper, I scraped all the dry mud off my legs and crawled fully clothed on to my mat, pulling my space blanket wearily over me.

7 CROCS AND INDIANS

I was up at first light on 18th August and rekindled the fire. A young Indian came to stand and stare at me from the settlement; he was clearly not happy about my presence. I assured him I would soon be passing on to Atalaya but he did not answer. About five minutes later he returned with a small water melon which he gave to me. I offered him some fishing line in return and that was the end of that problem.

So, after a breakfast of water melon, some very stale bread still left from Shepahua and a cup of tea, I was on my way. It was not a pleasant spot and I had no desire to stay. Twisted, fallen, long-dead trees covered the banks; drunkenly tumbled at odd angles with their boughs interlaced, they filled me with gloom. Some were upended, their roots to the sky; others leaned over the river to snag the unwary. The cloudy day and eerie silence added to the graveyard effect. By 1600 I was just about at the junction where the river Tambo joins the Ucayali; as I expected a great deal of turbulence, I pulled up on to a bank to remove the fin from the kayak.

Atalaya was a mile or two up the Tambo river and progress was slow as I struggled against the current. I estimated that it would take me about an hour to get there which meant that after purchasing what I needed, I would not have much time left for finding a camp site before dark. There was a smooth comfortable-looking sand bank at the junction of the two rivers, so I decided that would have to do for tonight; I could reach Atalaya tomorrow.

Using my paddle, I shaped out a good sleeping spot in the sand and built my bivvy shelter. After a lovely wash, I scrubbed my clothes and got a good fire going. It was wonderful to feel clean and fresh again. There was a small bay in front of the camp and this was a good spot to collect drinking water. With almost no turbulence the sediments settled from the water and made it relatively clear. Usually after collecting water, I had to wait an hour or so for it to settle out.

For supper, it was macaroni cheese and then I stretched out by the fire. The night was beautifully clear, and I lay there supremely content. It was never possible to relax like this in the rat race, even short holidays from work each year only provided a superficial taste of something different. Here, where I had no schedule to keep, I was able to take time to appreciate everything around me. All the things that seemed so important in the frenzy of competitive life held no significance here. I was eating well, sleeping well and seeing new things every day whilst undergoing a unique adventure. I felt truly extended with all my senses fully alert.

It remained dry all night and I slept well; sand made an excellent bed. By morning I was having second thoughts about going upstream to Atalaya; was it worth the effort? Oats, sugar and possibly some tinned food were the main things I needed, but I could manage with my freeze-dried packs plus fruit and eggs from the small villages along the way for a few more days. I checked the maps out; there were a couple of towns marked between here and Pucallpa, I should reach the first in a day or two. If the worst came to the worst, Pucallpa would be possible within a week or so and everything would be available there. I decided definitely to give Atalaya a miss.

I was on my way by 0830, the current remained strong for the first few miles and then tapered off. The first Indian village I stopped at, had only a woman and child in it, probably Campa Indians known to reside in the vicinity of the Tambo river. I tried taking some film but, as I approached, the woman ran off into the bush. A few miles further on, there was another camp, so I went up to see if they had anything to trade. This camp was empty except for a couple of dogs who kept barking; all the cooking pots were neatly hung up and a large pile of bananas were stored in one shelter. Perhaps the men were out fishing and the women tending crops in a jungle clearing. After taking some photos, I returned to the kayak. Myriads of butterflies seemed to be doing a dance along the beach; pure yellows and plain whites twisted and turned, skittering in and out of a much larger variety, covered with exotic spots and stripes. Periodically, they all settled on the mud in a tight group of less than one foot in diameter and then they would take off again and flutter around each other as if courting. They repeated their delicate waltz over and over again, so I was able to creep close. I wished I had brought a better quality movie camera with me: it was the first time in my life I had seen such a thing. After filming for a few minutes I returned to my kayak and moved on.

There was no activity on the river now, just that eerie silence, broken by the occasional animal call. By mid-afternoon I spotted another Indian camp just across the river and decided to try for bananas. As I approached the village, I noticed an Indian girl cleaning cooking pots at the river's edge. She never saw me and appeared to be in a trance. Quietly I paddled up to within thirty feet of her and then let the kayak drift. The lower part of her face was painted red with achiote, a powdery seed coating which, to the best of my knowledge, is only used for decoration. I guessed she must be in love as her thoughts were miles away in another world. The kayak gently nosed up on to the bank, just beneath her. She gave a yell and fled up the bank, cooking pots flying in all directions. Now I was in trouble. What would she say on reaching the village? I had no idea but I could not imagine it would be in my favour. It was no use going on as I had seen how quickly these people could get messages downstream using something between shouting and yodelling. I would have to defuse the situation before it got out of hand. I scaled the bank as quickly as possible, dressed only in a T-shirt and shorts with no weapon in my hands. By the time I reached the top, a group of Indians were already on the scene, many carrying machetes. I immediately smiled and opened my hands wide as if to say, "Don't worry. It's only me. I've got nothing to hide." The Indians slowed their pace and glanced over the bank at my kayak. Soon they were smiling. Only a gringo would own a stupid-looking boat like that. While the going was good, I asked about bananas and they agreed to trade me some. My next request to film the village was politely but firmly refused. So gringo paddled on, feeling grateful, with a little more experience to his credit.

About an hour before dusk, I found a good sandy beach and decided to make camp. There was a series of sand dunes nearby and it seemed unlikely that anybody lived there. I climbed to the top of the dunes and scanned in all directions.

No huts, no people and no give-away smoke from camp fires. This place would do fine. A little further up the beach three bamboo poles were stuck into the sand, the skeletal remains of a long-since-abandoned shelter. Just what I needed for my bivvy. They even had some stringy bark around them used as twine for tying together. They were longer than usual so I broke them down to make six smaller poles. After erecting the bivvy, I got the fire going and unloaded my gear. The sun was still up so, after a good wash and swim in the river, I stood on the beach to dry. A warm gentle breeze was blowing and the last rays of sunshine were being refracted through the water droplets of my eyelashes. It was a very pleasant wind-down to the day. Suddenly I looked up and saw a mean-looking Indian woman standing on top of the sand dune peering down at the bivvy. I grabbed a pair of underpants to try to look respectable, and wished her the time of day. She ran away without answering and I now began to wonder if the poles I had used for the bivvy had some religious significance or were perhaps a way of laying claim to an area, a form of tribal marking.

When I stopped to think about it, I was vaguely aware that these Indians were different from those I had met earlier and I had noticed similar poles sticking in the sand banks along the way all day but had not, until now, given the matter much thought. Although the majority of the Indians in the Ucayali valley were Shipibo, those that camped on the high ground had seemed more organised, better disciplined and a tidier bunch than those who dwelt in the low marshy areas. Those that I had met earlier had neat little thatched huts which were always clean and tidy with everything in its place and a place for everything; even their clothes, whether western or traditional Indian, were brighter and more decorative, whereas these marshy types were more scruffily dressed, frequently wearing the remnants of western clothes. They seldom combed their hair and lived in what could only be described as rather squalid inverted birds' nests amidst the cane grass.

As I had already unpacked the kayak, I would have to play it cool for she was sure to be back soon with assistance. I put my shorts on, and a clean white polo neck, climbed the sand dunes, and started gathering wood. About fifteen minutes later, back she came with two rugged-looking accomplices all on the trot and expecting trouble. I continued to gather wood until they were about fifty yards away when I raised my hand, waved and walked slowly towards them. Being unarmed was to prove the best weapon I had. I smiled and offered my hand in friendship. Surprisingly it was accepted. I lost no time in explaining that I was just passing through on my way to Pucallpa and led them over to my camp to show them the incredible gringo canoe. Soon they were grinning and I assured them yet again that I was just passing through. We shook hands once more and all was well.

It rained heavily that night and the bivvy sagged lower and lower, until it fell free of its tie points. The mosquitos were now becoming a nuisance; I had seen very little of them in the higher altitudes but now their numbers were increasing. I made numerous attempts throughout the night to re-secure the bivvy cover but it would not hold. Eventually, I gave up and yanked the space blanket over me as best I could. I spent a miserable night; sand seemed to stick to my damp skin whenever I rolled over. I would almost doze off when a sharp mosquito bite would bring me back fully awake, all too aware of my gritty wetness.

It was good to see the morning, at least the mosquitos had called their attacks off by then. A quick breakfast of porridge and I was on my way by 0800. By midday I reached a junction in the river. According to the map, there was a large island here, about five miles long and almost as wide. There did not seem any advantage in which channel I took as distances were about the same. However, the left-hand channel possibly had a town or a village about half-way down although these names on the map often meant nothing, perhaps the location of a hacienda in bygone days. The channel was very narrow, with steep banks on both sides. Crocodiles were in abundance, mostly small ones about three feet long. They would be dozing on a ledge or a bank as I rounded a bend in the river and, after waking up with a shock, they would throw themselves in the river. So long as big daddy was not around, there should be no problem. About half-way down the channel, I could hear somebody playing a harmonica. There was a small shelter on the right bank and a woman was swaying up and down in a hammock. I tied the kayak up and scaled the bank. There were chickens running around so, if I was lucky, I might get some eggs here. I called out to the woman in the hut, hoping to do some negotiating but she jumped out of her hammock and fled for the trees. There was a terrible fear of strangers here. She was almost certainly Indian but this was no Indian camp, across the river was a large house surrounded by open fields; maybe the woman or her husband worked for the owner of the estate. Someone across the river was yelling and shouting, about what I did not know, but I decided to give the place a miss.

A couple of miles downstream was another large estate, with a small motor boat tied up at the river's edge. This was a proper hacienda, perhaps I could trade here. Some Indian women, washing clothes at the water's edge, eyed me sceptically. I passed the time of day and one of the women went ahead of me to the main building where the owner's wife gave me a quick assessing glance and called to her husband. "Do you have eggs?" I asked. "I am on my way to Pucallpa." "Come in," he said, still eyeing me cautiously. "I'm on an expedition," I added. "Is this place Floresta?" "Yes," he replied and then called out to the woman working in the kitchen. "Where are you from?" he asked. "Australia," I said. He was most impressed. He sent one of his servants for a packet of biscuits and a bottle of rum. "Do you know what that is?" he asked. "Yes, rum," I replied, "but I don't drink." Next he produced an atlas and we browsed through it. "That's where I come from," I said, pointing at the map of Australia. He then produced a large notebook and asked me to fill in my name and address. "Will you send me a card when you return to Australia?" he asked. "Yes," I said, "certainly. Just give me your name and address." He wrote his name, Señor Hemen Cagna Figueroa, and an address in the next town, Bolognesi. "My grandfather was Italian," he said, pointing to his name. Soon fried fish, fried bananas and rice were laid on the table for me, along with a mug of hot milk. "Are you well armed?" he asked, mimicking firing a gun with his hands. "No, it's not necessary," I said, shrugging my shoulders. He shook his head at the wisdom of that. "There's lots of bandits, you know." I asked how long it took to get to Bolognesi. "About two hours by motor boat; about six by canoe," he said. I asked if it was a commercial town and he said, "Just a little." I had eaten well and soon he was yelling at the cooks to bring more. It is rather hard to act the gentleman (which of course you should be doing under such circumstances), when you have mounds of delicious food put in front of you and you are really hungry. But I think I managed reasonably well. I could feel some resentment from the Indian servants and cooks. Here was I, just passing in a canoe and getting all the VIP treatment. I think they believed it was because I was white and that this treatment would not have been given to an Indian. Another mug of milk and I was full.

So it was six hours to the next commercial town by canoe but since this was referring to a dugout, I figured I could do it in an hour or so less. I thanked Señor Figueroa for his kindness and promising again to send a card, waved farewell and was on my way.

Just after 1300, filled with plenty of calories, I decided to strike out for Bolognesi before dark. There were no difficult stretches, just the abundance of small crocs which by now I took no notice of. By 1700 I arrived and most of the town of Bolognesi came out to see me. I got six eggs at one store and tinned sardines, milk and coffee at the next. The second store was attached to the only hotel in town, the Hotel Municipal. Although the range of goods was small, it quite surprised me what they did have. The owner wiped dust off a solitary tin of butter. "Look, Australian," he said with pride. "Very good." It would have been an interesting story in itself, how that tin of butter got over 3000 miles up the Amazon. Also on sale were Alka Seltzer tablets and Milk of Magnesia. Perhaps they suffered from a lot of stomach problems in these parts. There was no sugar in the village and no oats, which rather disappointed me.

It was close to dark now, so I decided to book a room in the hotel. I unloaded the kayak and left it in the corridor. For 1000 soles a night, there was no mattress, no water and no lights. I found this acceptable in such a remote area but the general grottiness and untidiness I found harder to stomach. The whole town was much the same, empty cans and bottles thrown everywhere, people tended to urinate when and where they felt like it. Most Indian camps, by comparison, were tidy and free from foul odours and yet these town dwellers tended to look down on them. The store owner repeatedly warned me about the natives and told me how dangerous they were and not to trust them. "I am a mestizo," he would say. "You can trust a mestizo." I could have quoted him a list of examples to the contrary, but I did not see the point.

"Is there a restaurant in town?" I asked. He pointed to a shack attached to the hotel, but seemed to disapprove. "You'd possibly get something there," he said. After sorting my things out and still wearing my buoyancy vest, I walked into the restaurant. It was really a bar with a couple of wooden benches, a table and a home-made oil lamp for lighting. The only other customers were crew members off a small cargo vessel tied up here. They invited me over to join them for a drink but I politely declined. I asked one of the ladies working there if they had any cooked food. "We can give you some rice and beans," she said, "but that's all." "That's fine," I replied. I could see now why the store owner did not like recommending me here. The store owner was quite possibly gay and the young ladies were of a rather dubious virtue, so I guessed there was a clash of interests.

Next morning I was up early, despite a night interrupted by one of the crew men entertaining one of the ladies in the room next door. There was nowhere to get breakfast, so after a tin of milk and a tin of sardines, the kayak was loaded and I was ready for action. Most of the town came to see me off, including a police officer, possibly the only one here. I waved farewell and by 0745 I was on my way. Strong winds to contend with for most of the day and it made the going hard despite a one-knot current in my favour. Some friendly Indians called me over, so I stopped and took some group photos. Some of these people might have contacts with other groups further downstream and I considered it wise to keep on friendly terms with them. There is a grapevine on the river and it can either work for or against you. Just near Cumaria was another island, the main-stream going to the left and a narrow channel to the right. The narrow channel would probably give me protection from the wind so I decided to take it. With very little movement on the water, it was ideal croc country. A loud splash as I rounded a bend and off they scarpered. About half-way down the channel I was spotted by two Indian men and a young woman in a dugout canoe. They thought I had not seen them and pulled into the left bank using overhanging trees as camouflage. When I was within fifty yards of them, they pulled out and cut straight across my bow. I had to stop paddling to avoid a collision. They pretended not to see me and looked only straight ahead of them. I wished them the time of day and they returned the compliment, turning their heads as if it was the first time they had noticed me. "Where are you going?" one asked. "To Pucallpa," I replied. "Ah, Pucallpa," they repeated with smiles on their faces. To tell an Indian you were passing on always brought a smile to his face. Over the years they had seen their territory diminish in size so quite rightly they were suspicious of anyone in their region. As for their novel approach, I was to see this on numerous occasions during the trip. I got the impression that they intentionally put you in a position where you could not help noticing their presence. It is then your turn to start a conversation and explain yourself.

By 1600 I reached a sharp bend and although there was nothing marked on the map, there appeared to be a timber-milling town here, a fixed settlement of around 200 people. I scaled the earth bank, a fifty footer, to see what I could find. It was a mestizo settlement, not a company but a co-operative, I was told. The name of the place was San José.

"Is there a store here?" I asked.

"Not really but what do you want?"

"Some oats and some sugar."

"No sugar, but you can get oats in that building over there."

As it turned out, oats and beer were the only things sold here. After picking up a kilo of oats weighed on a dubious-looking set of scales and packed into an old plastic bag, it was time to move on. From the edge of the settlement I could get a good view of the river. There was a sandbank island less than a mile away and that would do for tonight.

The sandbank was fine except there was no driftwood on it. It was a fairly new bank, only a foot above the river and with no materials to make a bivvy. It looked like I would be sleeping in the kayak tonight. I had not yet slept in it, so it was worth trying. After supper, I pulled the kayak up to my selected sleeping spot, unscrewed the main front hatch and removed all the bulky items from this area. Next, I erected the canopy and fitted the mosquito net over it. Now I just had to slide in and fit my feet through the front hatch opening. My buoyancy vest and two air cushions improved the comfort, but it was not exactly paradise.

Mosquitos were able to break in and I got a poor night's rest. The eucalyptus oil I was using seemed rather ineffective. It smelt different from the Australian version, which worried me. Mosquitos would be getting more numerous from this point on and an effective deterrent was essential.

Winds were adverse again today and progress slow. I'd not loaded the kayak correctly and it was very sluggish. This, combined with the general lack of rest and sleep, did not make a very successful day for canoeing. Knowing where I was at any given time was largely a matter of guesswork. Often, I would be travelling in directions not marked on the maps. Alternative channels were frequently dried up and in some cases so overgrown with trees and vegetation they were almost impossible to spot. It was not hard to see why an accurate assessment of the Amazon's length was so difficult. It virtually changes length while you look at it. Large sections of the river's banks would slide into the river and get washed away. You could spot areas where settlements had existed just a year before by the banana palms and crumbling remnants of dwellings half-submerged in the river. In some parts, the undercutting action of the water was continuous and it was not wise to get too close to such banks where great crashes signalled the collapse of large sections and huge trees into the river.

I passed a great many Indian settlements during the day and was frequently called over. These people seemed to have more contact with the outside world than some of the earlier types I'd encountered; they were less suspicious of me. I now knew how to amuse them and established a good relationship. Just show the men the magnetic compass and the pump and let them feel the weight of the fibreglass paddle. For the ladies, who invariably wanted to know how I cooked, it was just as easy. Let them see a packet of freeze-dried food and my miniature billy can. "Only this," they would say, "only this?" Their cooking pots were big enough to put a human being in, and how I managed with a half-litre billy can, they could not understand. By 1600 I had had enough and pulled off the river. I decided to sleep in the kayak again that night.

After supper, I erected the canopy and a mosquito net over the cockpit area, using shock cord to secure its base to the deck. Improving comfort was less easy once in the cockpit, as there was little room for movement. The best position was lying on my back but, once in that position, I had to remain like that for the night.

I had a better night's sleep, but it was far from perfect. The mosquitos were still breaking in. The first job this morning was to get the washing done. Ideally, I tried to change my pants every day, my T-shirts or polo necks every two days, and about the same for my shorts. (I no longer wore gymshoes or socks; it was too difficult to keep them dry.) Conditions did not always permit this but I kept reasonably clean and tidy. Apart from feeling better for it, it also set an image that I was an expeditionary and not a hippy.

It was afternoon before I set off and I was not expecting a record today. I was now using the all-fibreglass paddle. Stony areas were very rare now so the white water paddle was no longer needed. After removing one of its blades, it was secured to the deck but could be removed rapidly if an emergency should occur such as the loss or breakage of the touring paddle.

At 1600 I passed an Indian and his wife in a motorised canoe. The husband was getting angry as the engine would not start. There was a small Indian settlement across the river and I guessed that was where they were aiming for. I pointed across the river and asked if their house was there. "Yes," they replied. I then produced some rope and offered to tow them across. They accepted and after fifteen minutes of strenuous effort, I reached the far bank. It was a good opportunity to get some photos, so I took my camera and scaled the bank. The husband and wife seemed to be the bosses of the settlement and were noticeably better off than the others. They had much better clothes and a quality shotgun and, of all things, an accordion. I had met the head man or the senior man of most villages I had stopped at and usually the difference between him and the others was not terribly significant. Apart from an air of importance, he did not seem a lot better off, but here the contrast was striking.

The group posed well and after taking a few group photos I was given a water melon and set off again. About half an hour later I pulled off the river and set up camp. Once more I tried sleeping in the kayak but, no matter what I did, the mosquitos would not be deterred.

By noon next day I reached a small village, San Louis, a good possibility for eggs and fruit, so I headed in to the beach. A large number of children were swimming and splashing about at the water's edge but as soon as they spotted me, they screamed and scrambled up the bank for all they were worth. This brought the elders out to see what was wrong. The first person to come down and see me was the village school teacher, Señor Moises Garcia Odicio. He introduced himself and asked where I was heading. I produced the map and showed him the general outline of my trip. "Ah, you're on an expedition," he said. "Yes," I answered, producing a camera, and asked if I could take some film of the village. "No problem," he said. By now the children of the village had plucked up enough courage to come back down to the beach and were smiling and giggling at my kayak. A couple of words from the school teacher about not handling the kayak and they all obediently stepped back. The village was Indian although a small trace of mestizo was visible in some of their faces. It was clean and tidy and well laid out. The children posed well as I filmed them and Señor Odicio proudly showed me his house and school – a thatched roof, sloping steeply down to within a few feet of the ground, wooden floors and no walls, just one blackboard and a couple of books. Children attended here until they were about twelve years old. Further education was possible in the larger towns such as Pucallpa and Lima. There was a large sack of government-supplied milk powder here and I was glad to see that some government assistance was reaching such remote areas. I asked about eggs and Señor Odicio turned to one of the children and asked, "Does your mother have eggs?" She was not sure but wandered off to find out. After exchanging addresses with the teacher, I was given a water melon and the young girl returned with one egg. "This is all there is at the moment," she said. "How much does your mother want for it?" I asked. She smiled and shrugged her shoulders. I gave her 500 soles, that's about five times the going rate, and a small donation to the school and made my way back to the beach.

The whole village watched as I pulled away. The children could not understand the kayak at all. So low at the water line – how did it stay afloat? They all screamed as it nosed through the first wave, believing it was all over for me there and then. Another scream but of less intensity, as it passed through the second, and an even smaller one as it made it through the third. Yes! This thing really floated, but they did not know how. I gave a wave and turned back downstream.

Winds were increasing now and a fair chop was picking up on the water. It was becoming overcast but I did not anticipate anything more than a small shower. That is how it started but before long it was pouring down and soon I was saturated. There was no point in stopping now so I just kept going. Half an hour later, it was all over and the sun was shining again. Most areas of the Amazon Basin receive from 80 to 120 inches of rain a year, so I couldn't expect to escape some wettings although it was the so-called dry season.

At 1600 I was called into a small Indian settlement near Iparia. The camp fires were burning, the supper was being cooked and I was feeling lucky, so I went in.

As expected, a crowd gathered to see the gringo machine and some asked if I had cigarettes. I offered them coffee instead and they wanted me to eat with them. It was a small group, mostly young couples in their twenties. The women continued to prepare supper, while the men asked me about myself. They had no idea where Australia was but guessed that it was a long way off. They asked if I had a family and I said, "Oh yes," and produced a photo of my cousin. The men looked it over and gave a few smiles and then the women came over and grabbed it from them. They looked it over carefully, gave a few grunts, and handed it back. In retrospect, I realised it was a mistake. The ladies here would never visit a hairdresser's or beauty parlour in their lives and here was my cousin with her hair done in long curls and make-up on, looking most attractive. It caused some jealousy.

We sat on the ground for supper, which was boiled bananas

and fish. I was a privileged guest and given a separate bowl. The other men ate from a communal bowl and the women sat by the fire eating what was left in the cooking pots. After supper, the men thanked the senior man of the group, and retired to their huts. Why they thanked him I do not know. All the men worked in these communities and all the women helped to prepare supper. But there must have been some special obligation to him.

A couple of miles downstream, I found a sandbank to camp on and started to gather wood. A few minutes later, three Indians, scruffily dressed in western clothes, passed by. They pretended not to see me so I called over to them. It was important to make my case now, and not have them visit me in the middle of the night to find out who I was. It appeared to be a father and two teenage sons, one of whom had a shotgun which was very old and held together with bits of string, carelessly slung over his shoulder. This general appearance did not inspire confidence. I explained to the father that I was just passing through and would be spending the night here. "No problems?" I asked. "No problems," he replied. I gave him a handful of fish hooks and they wandered off. That night I kept my flashlamp, knife and a stout stick in easy reach. I was not convinced that I would not be getting a midnight caller.

I was up at 0600. There had been no night visitors but the mosquitos played hell. The problem was now serious. Either they were getting through the net or under the sides as I rolled over in the night. The two Indian brothers returned, shotgun still slung carelessly over the elder one's shoulders. They wanted some fishing hooks too, so I gave them some hoping to get rid of them but they continued to hang around while I wrote the log and repacked my gear. One of them decided to sit in the kayak's cockpit and swing the paddle around as if he was rowing. Something was going to get broken, so I told him to get out. This upset them a bit and they started dropping hints about me leaving. "Yes, I'll be leaving soon," I informed them, and continued packing the kayak. They slowly wandered off.

I was hoping to replenish my supplies at the town of Iparia about three hours downstream, but – as it turned out – Iparia was no longer on the river. Either the river had changed course leaving it inland or perhaps it was only accessible by river in the wet season. A local informed me that it could be reached by foot in fifteen minutes but I decided against it. My kayak might not be here when I got back. It was a bit of a disappointment.

Half an hour later, I passed two mestizos in dugout canoes, just drifting downstream. They were mixed Indian and Negro. "Where are you heading?" I asked. "To Pucallpa," they replied. It was not unusual to find canoes loaded up with fruit and tradeable items drifting downstream in that direction but all these two had was a small bunch of bananas between them. Also at the rate they were travelling, it would be over a week before they reached Pucallpa.

Further downstream I pulled in to a small cove for a snack, just a couple of bananas and a drink of water. The two mestizos drifted past as I was studying my map. The next large town was probably Masisea and that was about three days' travel. Perhaps I would just be lucky and pick up some more eggs and fruit before that. I folded the map and started out, when I spotted one of the mestizos. He had crept along the bank almost to where I was resting and his intentions were obvious. The second mestizo was about fifty yards further down, where a small Indian village was located; he was eyeing the area and making sure no one was around so he could go in and steal. When things like that happened, travellers like me got the blame. If I had had a shotgun handy, I would have put their canoes out of action and left them to explain their presence to the Indians.

Towards evening in the vicinity of Venesia, I came across a rather large Shipibo Indian settlement, on a bluff forty feet above the river. The senior man of the village came forward and I introduced myself, after explaining where I was going, and asked if they had eggs or fruit for trade. They brought me two eggs and a water melon but did not seem terribly concerned about the price. They were on the edge of the money economy, so I gave them 1000 soles, which was well above the market value. One of the women was making bracelets. It was beautiful work, woven with tiny beads and had required a lot of patience. There was the usual assortment of pots and pans and wooden bowls around the camp and one toy for the kids to play with: a short plank of wood with one cross member at the end forming an axle and two pieces of hollowed bamboo for wheels. "And what's this?" I asked. "A car," they said, all laughing. "Where do you sleep?" they asked. I pointed to a sandbank down the river.

"There."

It was a fairly new sand bank with little flotsam lying around as yet. The wood I could find was damp and getting a fire going difficult. Mosquito swarms were forming as darkness fell and I was getting dizzier and dizzier blowing into the fire to try and keep it going. When I looked up, a long dugout was pulling in to the beach with no less than nine people on board – what's gringo done now? Nothing – it seemed the river grapevine was working once more and word was out that gringo is OK. They were smiling and carrying bowls of boiled bananas and fried fish. They gathered round my kayak and went through the usual questions; the pump, the compass and the paddle for the men and, of course, the cooking utensils for the ladies. Predictably, they roared as they picked up the billy can with sawn-off fork and spoon inside. We chatted for about fifteen minutes and then they handed me their food. I thanked them, gave them the remainder of my instant coffee and they paddled back across the river.

Strong winds next morning bore long lines of smoke upstream from where the Indians were burning new clearings. It is easy to spot the areas of former settlements along the river banks, even when they have been abandoned for years. A different shade of green is first observable at about a mile distant. A variation of tree and scrub height is the next indication, and then the unmistakable sign of the now-exhausted banana palms being choked by the jungle growth around them. So long as the soil is given enough time to recuperate, no permanent damage will be done.

By 1230 I reached Conchurri, an Indian-style settlement but the inhabitants were mostly mestizos. A small cargo vessel, the RM *Axel* from Pucallpa, was tied up here. I asked the crew if there was a store, but they shook their heads. "There's a pension here," one said, "if you want to stay over-night." Another crew member called me up to the top of the bank, indicating I could get a meal there. It seemed like a good idea.

The pension was almost exclusively for ships' crews staying over and meals were probably included in the price. It was very basic, just a few huts with hammocks suspended from the walls. The crew introduced me to the owner, a wise-looking woman of about fifty. "Could I eat here?" I asked. "Yes," she replied. Knowing the shortage of change they have in these places, I asked if she had change of 1000 soles. Her answer was something to the effect of, "Don't worry, I'll get rid of that for you," and everybody laughed.

First I was given a large mug of delicious fruit juice, a real luxury in those parts, and then boiled bananas, chicken and spaghetti, which was most filling. "How much?" I asked the owner. She shook her head saying, "Nothing." Did I have a camera? she asked. I went to get it. After taking a few group photos, I asked a crew member to write me the address of the place. "They don't have one," he answered. "In another year they'll move on from here." "How about if I sent the photos to your company in Pucallpa; might you see this woman again?" "It's possible," he said, giving me the address. These people seemed to live very close to the Indian way of life, moving on to a new settlement every year. Cargo vessels around a hundred tons (such as was here today) might call a few times each year to do some trading and that was about the limit of contact with the outside world.

"Show me what that thing can do," the woman said, pointing at the kayak. Fair enough, so before I moved on I took it out to midstream, paddled it forward at full speed, did some emergency stops, spun it around and paddled it backwards.

At 1630 I located a suitable sandbank and made camp, burying the bottom edges of the mosquito net in the sand to prevent the mosquitos getting under the sides. But by dawn next morning it was quite obvious that theory does not always accord with practice. There were at least a hundred blood-filled mosquitos inside the net with me, trying to get out. I examined it carefully and could not find any major holes or openings. The mesh of the net was not of the finest weave and the only possible way that they could be getting in was by forcing their way through it. After filling up with blood, they then had the problem of getting back out and the racket they made was like a squadron of Spitfires. The problem was serious as I was getting less and less sleep at nights and this would soon wear me down.

95

That morning, I charged the flashlamp batteries and wrote letters to family. I also started a shopping list of things I would need in Pucallpa. Pucallpa was a large town with a population of 55,000 people and should have everything I needed. Mosquito repellent was, of course, top of the list, as was a one-man tent. If I could find such a thing, I could dump the space blanket to make room for it. I had used a fair few packs of freeze-dried foods by now, so there was a little more space. I would need a new notebook as they were very handy both for writing letters in and as a source of toilet paper.

I checked my maps and estimated I should reach Masisea today – it was about thirty miles off. At 1015 I was under way and by 1315 I had got as far as the mestizo town of Santa Rosa. As I arrived the wind suddenly increased to gale force and the paddle was almost ripped from my hands. The only warning I had was to see a dust storm gathering downstream. Within a couple of minutes, it was on me and it took a considerable effort to reach the bank.

Within fifteen minutes it had passed and I scaled the bank to the town which was as grotty as they come. It seems that the larger the number of permanent buildings, the more the town grows, the greater the squalor. There were a couple of small stores selling grain, salt, milk and sugar. I drank one tin of milk while I waited and asked the store owner where I should put the empty tin. "Under the house," I was told. No wonder there was a fetid odour here. Pigs, dogs, ducks and a variety of other animals roamed around the streets, fouling the place up and most people walked around bare foot. I bought a few tins of milk, six eggs, half a kilo of sugar and on to Masisea which was certain to be larger and would offer a greater range of goods.

Masisea looked rather beautiful from the river, not unlike a Cornish village; a narrow cliff line, rich green grass and small bungalows. I drifted in midstream for a while taking photos. There was a floating store at one end of town supplying fuel and tinned food. This was the best range of goods I had seen on the trip so far and so it was time to spend-up: a kilo of oats, a tin of Nescafé, a tin of chocolate milk powder, a bar of soap, a tin of cheese, and a tin of Vick which I hoped would repel the mosquitos as it contained camphor.

The Urubamba starts as a precipitous boulder-strewn stream above Machu Picchu.

The one hotel at Bolognesi, but it stocked Australian butter.

Boys on a balsa wood raft at Fortaliza.

Policeman and trusty at the Colonia Penal del Sepa checkpoint.

Beach camp, everything to hand.

Two charming sisters at Pucallpa.

An Indian settlement among the rice paddies between Sheshea and San Luis.
Posing for the group photograph involved a lot of consultation.

Beneath wide skies. Above, fish drying, and below, Indian territorial marker wands which I learnt not to use as camp pegs.

Preparing dried fish to take down river to Iquitos.

The farm workers in the rice paddies.

Masisea looked beautiful from the river.

Peanut farm workers come to inspect the gringo canoe.

Amazon river craft: above, small cargo vessel at Conchurri; below, fishing boats at Cabo Maguari.

Journey's end at Cabo Maguari.

It would have been a change to have had a browse round to see what Masisea was like close up, but finding a sleeping spot was a higher priority right now, so with half an hour of sunlight left, I pushed on a mile downstream to a large sandbank. Turkey buzzards were in abundance, picking up fish scraps left behind by fishermen. They were no problem and it was good of them to clean the place up for me.

For supper, I managed to get through most of the tin of cheese, followed by some porridge and boiled eggs. A rare mix, but very filling. Unfortunately, being so greedy tended to make me sweat more, aggravating the mosquito problem. I covered myself with Vick, rolled up in the space blanket with the mosquito net laid on top. The mosquitos still gave me hell: effective solutions would now have to wait until Pucallpa.

Next day I paid for overeating. My stomach was feeling like a lump of lead. I tried working it off by canoeing.

A well-loaded motor canoe pulled out from an island and appeared to be following me. After about thirty minutes, they pulled alongside and asked where I was going. I didn't know what to make of them. One man had blond hair and a face as red as a tomato, the other was heavily bearded, and there was a local-looking girl with them. It turned out that they were a pair of German gringos who had long since abandoned the western way of life. The bearded one claimed to be a doctor and the blond a jungle tour operator out of Pucallpa. Their girlfriend was a Colombian. Apparently the tourist business was rather flat at the moment and they had been upstream buying fruit and hunting. They now planned to sell this produce in Pucallpa. "We've heard about you all up the river," said one. "The Indians told us about this fantastic red and white gringo canoe that was made of aluminium." (It seems the fibreglass explanation I was giving had been misunderstood.) "What happened to your face?" I asked the blond one. "It's red dye I got from the Indians," he said. "They told me it protected the skin from the sun." I could not help thinking that perhaps the Indians had a good sense of humour; he certainly looked hilarious with it on. I took some movie film of them and we parted company.

Towards evening, a young man called me over to the bank where he was standing. I was suspicious but decided to see what he wanted. He told me this was a river control point and started to check the cargo out, handling everything roughly. I pushed him away and asked to see his credentials. He put on a stupid grin – he knew he had been caught. I was sorely tempted to give him a good hiding but for the possibility of damaging the kayak.

Sunday, 29th August was a foggy day. I was not very happy with the camp site, so at 0615 I pushed on downstream. The fog was thick and at times I could see neither bank. This was where the compass proved its worth. It could not tell me where the bends were, but at least I would not be going back upstream. There was very little movement on the water to tell you which way was downstream.

At 0800 the fog lifted and a fine day was apparent. I reached a large island and could not decide which way to go round it and my maps were unable to give any clues. The maximum flow appeared to be going to the right, so I followed this channel. Five miles later and after my compass had passed through 210 degrees, I knew I had lost on the deal. The left-hand channel would have got me there in half a mile. How I longed for quality maps.

By mid-morning I had arrived at a small mestizo village with a floating service station at the edge and who should be tied up here but the German gringos. The store owners came out and asked the Germans who I was. "He wants to know if this is the American Embassy," the German replied. At that the store owners doubled up with laughter. I tied ol' kayak up and the store owners cooked me a breakfast of chicken and rice.

It was mostly flat water to Pucallpa and the sun really glared. By 1730 I was in the dock area and looking for a place to leave the kayak. I expected the shopping would take a day to complete, so I needed somewhere safe for my equipment; I spotted a marina and decided to give it a try. A teenage girl was running the show and said she would speak to her father. The river flowed strongly here and the marina was floating on large logs, secured to the bank by heavy cables. The purpose of these 'floating' marinas, service stations and stores was to compensate for the annual rise and fall of the river, which here was about six metres. Most of the marina's boats were small, motorised canoes, rented to locals for fishing trips.

The father agreed to let me stay, so an old man gave me a hand to pull the kayak up on to the marina. I told the father about my expedition and he was most impressed. "You can sleep here, if you want to," he said, pointing at one of the rooms. I mentioned that I needed some supplies and asked which direction the stores were. "One of my daughters" (he had seven) "will take you downtown later," he said. He was later to change his mind about this and sent the night-watchman instead.

The two eldest daughters gave me a hand to unload all the gear from the kayak. It was going to be locked up for safe-keeping while I was down town. They thoroughly enjoyed themselves. "What's this for? What's that for?" and "How do you use this?" Then, when they saw something they liked, it was, "Present for me, Gringo?" They were in their early to mid teens and both were very attractive. When they found the cameras, they naturally wanted photos taken. The eldest daughter picked up the movie camera at arm's length and, pointing towards herself, started running it. She pretended just to be interested in how it worked – I forgot to tell her that there was no film in it!

The old man who had helped me pull my kayak up also appeared intrigued by my equipment and his excessive interest worried me. The eldest daughter noticed this and discreetly asked if he was with me. "No," I said. "I thought he worked here." She shook her head. He was just hanging around waiting for opportunities. Fifteen minutes later the family called me over to join them in a soft drink. Most of the valuable cargo was now loaded into the holdalls so I sat down with them. We chatted a bit about my trip but, after a couple of minutes, I excused myself just to see what the old man was up to. He was gone and so was my camper mat. I was most annoyed. Its value was only about $10 but, like most other things I had, it was essential equipment. The father offered to pay for it, but I told him that the price was not significant.

The watchman took me downtown for the evening. Using a flashlamp we made our way through the unlit riverside slums, the shantytown that appears at the end of every wet season as the river recedes. Past the makeshift bars where young prostitutes ply their trade. "Five hundred's the price," (seventy cents

US) said the watchman. "And *muchos problemas mañana*," I replied. To this he laughed.

Few stores were open downtown and, as luck would have it, the next day was a national holiday. I made some enquiries at jungle tour operators in town as to whether any camping equipment was available. "None at all," I was told.

Monday morning I raced around town as some of the shops would be open for a few hours. Since I could not get a tent, I decided to make a sleeping-sack out of heavy-gauge cotton to keep the mosquitos off me. I purchased four metres of the heaviest gauge material I could find, some needles, cotton and scissors. To replace the camper mat, I bought two metres of polythene sheet.

Next I needed a few clothes as my polo necks were beginning to fray and my two pairs of underpants would not last forever. So I purchased three more polo necks and one more pair of pants. I was hovering at the window of a fashionable boutique trying to spot a cheap pair of jeans, when the owner virtually pulled me inside. I told him about my trip and the problem I was having with mosquitos. He folded up an expensive pair of jeans and gave them to me. "Just sign this book and send me a postcard from Australia," he said. Things were going well and it was not lunch time yet. I managed to get some insect repellent that looked like deodorant sticks, and some Iodine for water purification. I still had plenty of purification tablets left but I was getting through much more water than I'd expected in the heat.

At the supermarket, I bought milk powder, tea, sardines and a notebook. I spent a long time here browsing through a range of machetes; they would make very effective weapons but their weight and bulkiness was a drawback. I had got this far with no problems so I decided to give them a miss. The post office would be open tomorrow and since I had some films to send, I decided to stay another night.

I joined the family for lunch and they made me feel at home. The marina owner's brother came to see him and he spoke English. He warned me of the area between here and Iquitos and told me some horrific stories. He was a serious, sensible man and there was no reason why he should lie to me. But the kind of stories he told me are sometimes better not to know. Apparently there were frequent murders along the river and bodies were found with their faces cut out. "Is there some cult or tribal significance attached to this?" I asked. He didn't know the reason but he knew that it went on.

I spent the afternoon making my sleeping-sack, much to the amusement of the two eldest daughters. "How much were your jeans, Gringo?" asked the eldest daughter. "A present," I said, and she burst out laughing, uncertain whether to believe me or not.

By evening my stomach was demanding food again and so I went downtown for a steak, some mixed fruit and a lot of icecream that I had so often dreamed about under that blazing sun. After that I returned to the marina and climbed into my hammock, slung just above the kayak, in case someone decided to try to run off with it in the night.

Next morning, after I had posted some films and changed some more money, I inscribed my name in the family book and I was on my way. "*Bon voyage* and take care, Gringo," they called.

An hour later I ran into a heavy downpour but decided to keep going. I wanted to get well clear of the town and back into the clean living of the jungle. I had dysentery again, no doubt from eating in the restaurants. The kayak was sluggish and would need rebalancing. There were a few extra kilos of cargo to contend with now.

Half an hour before sunset I pulled up on to a bank and made camp. I was rather anxious to check my sleeping-sack out to see if I had solved the mosquito problem. After supper of eggs and sardines I covered all my exposed areas of skin with insect repellent and crawled into the sack. The insect repellent could not be used above the shoulders as the odour it gave off was dangerous to inhale. My arms and legs were not getting bitten but logically my face was suffering. Also, being in the sack tended to make me sweat more and this really brought the mosquitos in swarms. I tried covering my face with a bush hat and then a layer of mosquito net over this, and sweated all the more.

Just as I was dozing off, I felt a thump on the sack. My first thought was a snake, and I was out of that sack like a rocket. But it was only a frog which seemed almost tame. I checked around the camp and spotted a great many. They were not the poisonous type and so I got back into my sack. The frogs did not worry about me at all and were soon hopping all over me. One thing that became apparent was a noticeable decline in mosquitos. Whether I was working as a team with the frogs I did not know but it was quite possible that they were eating the mosquitos that I was attracting. I could sometimes hear the drone of a mosquito as it moved towards my face. It seemed to get within a couple of inches and then abruptly vanish. Also, since the frogs were hopping around so openly, I guessed there could not be any snakes in the vicinity.

A fair night's sleep but room for improvement. The dysentery worsened but I did not anticipate any long-term problems. I spent the morning drying clothes and rebalancing the kayak. It was a midday take off again and a heavy downpour within the hour – a repetition of yesterday. My nylon spray jacket was only showerproof and it was not long before I was soaked through. The ideal protection would have been the plastic poncho; with the hood on and the cape end spread over the cockpit area, I would have been virtually waterproof but it would have acted like a sail to the strong winds and could have caused me to capsize; trying to swim with that on would be both difficult and dangerous. I tried it once but the risk was too high.

By 1700 I reached a mestizo village called Tacshitea. There was probably a population of around 400, but no mention of it on my maps. I decided to give the pension a try. It was very basic with a raised wooden floor and bamboo poles for walls, run by a quietly spoken woman with two children, who were also very quiet and very respectful.

A large crowd of kids followed me up to the pension, anxious to see the kayak. I laid it in the hallway and told them to take care. It was glass fibre, I said, and I rapped the shell with my knuckles to let them hear the sound. Predictably, every kid in turn rapped it with his knuckles and turned to his friend saying, "Glass fibre." After fifteen minutes of this, the pension owner told them they would have to go as they were letting all the mosquitos in.

Just before dusk, the whole village wandered down to the river for a wash, the men in their shorts and the women in dresses. There was nowhere private enough to wash without your clothes on, and logically enough no other running water but the Amazon in a village on the river. The usual practice is to wade out to where the water is just three feet deep, sit down with your clothes on and throw water over yourself. Then it's back to the village and put some dry clothes on. The Indians always bathe naked and that is how I prefer it.

I joined the pension family for a supper of egg, rice and chicken. There was no husband present and the mother gave the impression of being a widow. Apart from a midnight dash to the WC (a pit in the back garden) I slept well. Almost no mosquitos, but why? There was a great gap between the top of the walls and the thatched roof. They could come in by their millions, if they so desired. So what stopped them?

It was egg, beans and rice for breakfast, followed by a coconut off the garden tree. I packed my gear and asked how much I owed. "It is up to you," she said. I gave her 5000 soles and reasoned that she could use the extra. She handed me the family book and I signed my name.

At 0900 I was in my kayak and ready to leave. The family came down to see me off. "Don't forget your hat, Alan," said the mother. "The sun is very strong today. Take care."

There were a few showers, but generally it was a good day for canoeing. Some logging was going on in the area but it was hard to perceive the magnitude of the operation from the river as much of the deforesting occurred further inland; with tracks being built to drag the lumber to the water's edge. About twenty per cent of the Amazon jungle has now vanished, which greatly concerns the world's environmentalists.

Maps were of little use again today as channels had dried up or changed course and I had to play it by sight with hopefully not too many extra miles.

By evening my estimated position was Alfonso Ugarte and I set up camp. The mosquito problem was the worst yet and there seemed no answer to it. The needles jabbed me in the back as I carried a scalding billy of water, or in the arm as I was trying to cut some wood with my knife. I could stand in the smoke of the fire until I almost choked but nothing would deter them. Unable to sleep at night I would pace up and down beating off swarms of them with a T-shirt, finally falling asleep from sheer exhaustion. By dawn all uncovered parts of my body and face felt like the surface of orange peel.

Night canoeing could be dangerous but it was worth considering. So long as there was an air flow over the body, mosquitos tended not to settle.

The next night the moon was full and I canoed until 2000 when the sky clouded over and the wind picked up, making it dangerous, so I pulled off the river and waited. By 2130 the moon was bright again and the wind dropped. It was quite enjoyable and being out of the blazing sun made canoeing easier. Schools of startled fish jumped clear of the water and in one case I received a wet smack across the face. By 2200, the channel narrowed, the sky clouded again and I could hear rushing water. There was either a rapid or a major obstruction in the river. The river seemed to be flowing against me so I stopped paddling and eyed the tree-line to try and work out my direction of drift. Yes, I was going backwards, but why?

There is a phenomenon that occurs in the Amazon. When water levels in a tributary are lower than in the mainstream, the flow will be reversed. That was the situation I now believed I was in. Instead of taking an alternative channel around an island, I believed I had found my way up a tributary. I was being dragged out to midstream, a slight spin and I was moving forward again. Now I had the picture. There was a large obstruction of dead trees to the right side of the river which turned the flow around in a giant eddy. You could either keep drifting round with this and hopefully not get caught in the trees or do as I did, drift further across the river and reconnect with the main flow. The skies cleared again and the moon shone brightly, so I paddled on.

By 2400, my wrist was aching so it was time to rest. There was a large flat sand area to my left and that would do for camp. I nosed ol' kayak into the beach and took my flashlight to inspect the site. About 500 yards away there seemed to be some sheets flapping in the wind. The Indians often left hammocks and blankets out to air during the daytime but I had never seen them at night. Also, since there was no wind, why were they flapping? Whatever it was, I wanted to find out. I do not doubt the existence of supernatural things but I have no reason to fear them. If I did, I would not be canoeing the Amazon by myself.

After walking forward another twenty yards I realised what had happened and returned to the kayak. Yes, its white sides twisted and moved too. I had experienced this phenomenon once before some years back. If you keep looking at a moving effect such as the twisting, warping reflection of the moon on water for a couple of hours and then try to focus your eyes on something static, the stationary object tends to take on the warping motion for a few minutes. A similar experience can be had by looking over the stern of a ship for half an hour or so, at the propellers turning and twisting the water in all directions, then trying to look at a fixed object. This will almost certainly appear to move or, alternatively, you will be violently sea-sick. I took another look in the direction of the sheets and realised that they were the white bark of a perfectly motionless group of trees.

Conspicuous by their absence were the mosquitos. But why? What was different? What rules do they keep? Does a full moon have anything to do with it? There must be a pattern. Was it possible they had selected their victims long before this time, got their fill of blood and returned to base?

After breakfast on 4th September, I wrote letters to the Explorers' Club and my family to post at the next large town, Contamana. By 1000, the sand was scorching my feet and so I got under way. The sky was clear, the water glassy calm and the sun glared at me. My beard growth was thick enough to protect my lips and most of my face but my nose was really going through it in an almost constant state of peeling. The spray cover protected my legs but made the cockpit area rather sweaty.

By 1400 I had reached Contamana which was reasonably tidy at the centre but grotty at the river's edge. All the refuse was thrown down the river bank to stink and rot. Most of the people were decent enough and I just could not understand why they could not organise a better rubbish-disposal system.

A large crowd gathered around the kayak and asked questions about the expedition. There was a restaurant at the top of the bank so I ordered a couple of egg sandwiches and sat down where I could watch the kayak. The crowd had dispersed now but one undesirable-looking character was still hanging around. I just sat down there and watched him until he could no longer justify his presence and left. I paid the restaurant owner's son to watch the kayak for me while I did a little shopping. He stood by the kayak making sure there were no souvenir hunters. It was something I hated doing because it is almost like saying that you did not trust anybody in town, but what other choice did I have? My equipment was essential and much of it irreplaceable. Without it the expedition would come to an abrupt halt.

Contamana was fairly large and offered a reasonable range of goods. I bought some more cotton cloth for a sleeping-sack modification and also a larger, heavier three-quarters-of-a-litre billy can and some more eggs, oats, chocolate milk powder and tinned food.

Half an hour before sunset, I was once more on my way. It was a beautifully clear evening; ideal for night canoeing. So long as there is enough light to miss the obstacles, it can be most enjoyable although it required a higher degree of concentration, since obstacles like semi-submerged logs were not always visible until I was within a couple of yards of them. A great splash across the bow, breaking the silence of night could make my heart miss a beat or two, as I almost collided with a large fish or crocodile.

Picking a camp spot was, of course, more dangerous at night: snakes are hard enough to spot by day with their expert camouflage, let alone in the dark, but if I was lucky I would find a sandbank whose bright, smooth surface would be lit by moonlight so that any discontinuity, such as a snake, stood out. A snake could, however, take on the appearance of a piece of driftwood so if I was unsure, I would poke the object with my paddle just to check it out. I had had enough experience with crocodiles now to know their favourite habitats; fortunately, it was not exposed sandbanks.

By 2230, I'd had enough. My wrist was aching again and I did not want to aggravate the problem. The skies were still clear and so I did not bother making a shelter. I laid my plastic poncho out on the ground and flopped down on top of it in my sleeping-sack.

Sunday, 5th September was sleeping-sack modification day. I decided to make a hood for it with just a small breathing and seeing vent at the front, in order to keep the mosquitos away from my face. This task took me until 1400. By then, a storm was brewing but I decided to move anyway, keeping close to the bank just in case things got out of hand. It was nothing too serious so I kept going.

By 1700 I reached an Indian village and tried for bananas. By now I had learnt that many Indians called them *platana*; I'd probably missed out on them in some places by using the wrong word. These were Shipibo again, about forty people, and very likeable. One of the girls was out in midstream trying to prove to her father how well she could handle a canoe. There was a bend on the river here and quite a bit of turbulence. There was no doubt about it, she really could handle that canoe. A great variety of strokes in and out of the turbulence, and some beautiful hip movements that I could not help noticing. The only thing that puzzled me was that she was so well dressed. What was the special occasion? Dad seemed happy with the performance and nodded approval. Another young lady, also in her late teens, climbed into the canoe and they took off downstream.

Yes, they had bananas to trade. How many did I want? I held up ten fingers and off they went to get them. If you just said bananas, they were apt to bring you a bunch big enough to sink the kayak. Now came the usual questions about where I was going, where I was from and where do I sleep at nights. There was always a good laugh when I would point to a sandbank and say, "My bed is here." I was living more basically than they were. A few more minutes and I was on my way.

A mile or two downstream, I spotted the two young ladies in

the canoe. They did not seem to be going anywhere, just drifting around in an eddy. As I got closer, the full picture emerged. Some Indian youths from another village were up on a bank calling out to them. It was courting time and the girls were playing a little game of hard to get, paddling around in circles. For a moment I thought about my chances, but then again who would want a thirty-eight-year-old bearded gringo who slept on sandbanks?

By 1800, navigation was getting difficult. There was no moon and the river was running strongly here. I was close to a good bank so I decided to give night canoeing a miss and make camp.

After supper, I relaxed by the fire and thought about the Indians. There would not be many of them from here on and I was rather sorry. After all the terrible stories I had heard about them I had found very little to substantiate such tales: they could have robbed me and cut my throat a thousand times. I was still here and nothing I had lost could be blamed on them.

I guess the missionaries mean well but these people need nothing from us. They are not short of food, they are happy, with no unemployment, drug or alcohol problems. Take a stroll through the slums and ghettos of our cities and see if we can claim the same.

9 AFTER THE INDIANS

Monday, 6th September, I awoke at dawn feeling relaxed and well-rested. No mosquitos during the night, but why not? Could this be the start of the dry season in this region and had I spent a lot of time making a sleeping-sack for nothing? Or was there some vegetation or odour around here that was disagreeable to them?

It was porridge for breakfast and on my way by 0800. There were rarely any lunch stops, perhaps just a couple of bananas and some water while I drifted. By 1600 I had passed Orellana and pulled on to a bank to prepare for night canoeing. This involved securing the flashlamp within easy reach, refilling my water bottle and having a meal.

At 1730 I was under way but soon forced into a bank by strong winds. When they dropped I paddled on, but the moon would not be up for another couple of hours and the situation soon became hopeless; a cloudy sky and just a sprinkling of starlight. The winds picked up and I was forced back in to the bank again. There was nothing to do but to sit and wait.

There was a solitary hut on the shoreline, and somebody had spotted me. The white sides of the kayak were apt to reflect even the smallest amount of light. A couple of people came down to the beach scanning a flashlight around. They never came closer than fifty yards but they knew I was there and it bothered them. They returned to the hut and started banging on an oil drum and shouting. Perhaps they thought I was an evil spirit and had to be driven away.

By 2230, the moon was spreading enough light between the clouds for me to move. It was not good enough for safe night canoeing so I stopped off at the first camp I found. I never bothered with a shelter, just a plastic groundsheet and sleeping-bag.

I woke again at 0430 next morning. The moon was shining brightly now. There was no driftwood on the bank so it was better to move on. By 0730 I found a good bank and got breakfast organised. There was boiled egg, porridge and tea. I then spent a couple of hours relaxing, writing my log and sharpening my knife. After a late morning cup of coffee I was once more on my way. Winds were picking up again, but progress was fair – about five knots. By 1500 I had reached the small mestizo village of Ramon Castilla and stopped off for some trading.

I had developed the skill, in trading with these villages, of assessing the population and working out their likely spare-egg capacity. For example, if the population was less than fifty people, it would be pointless to ask for more than two eggs. They just would not have the surplus, so would say they had none to sell. So, I graded places as one, two or three eggers and usually won out. Another essential requirement was having plenty of small change. I could not expect a 5000-sol note to be acceptable in a place that was almost outside the money economy.

I made camp at 1700 and got some washing done. The moon would not be up for hours yet so night canoeing was out. It was sardines and water melon for supper. The bananas were getting less numerous in these parts. It is possible that the mestizos had a preference for water melon.

The mosquitos were back and in great numbers, so what was it they particularly liked about this place? The camp spot was typical, just a dry sandbank on a small island in the river, but they would not leave me alone. It was midnight before I finally got to sleep. The next day I decided to cut the front of the hood of my sleeping-sack right back to my forehead and cover the gap with three layers of mosquito netting. After climbing into the sack I would pull the hood over my head so that the mosquito net would cover the area between my forehead and neck. A reasonable-sized breathing area was necessary to avoid excessive sweating.

By 1130 it was a blistering hot day, well into the nineties. All my clothes were dry now. It was time to go. By 1500 I was near Dos de Mayo, a town that had probably once been on the river but was now well inland. I saw nothing of it as I passed. The sun glared at me all day and I had to make repeated applications of block-out cream to my nose and the backs of my hands. I wore a hat and sunglasses continuously and also a long-sleeved cotton polo neck. The polo necks were something that I had initially had doubts about bringing but they proved their worth. Having a sun at this intensity beaming on the back of my neck for hours on end was inviting trouble. Even the well-seasoned locals wore wide-brimmed hats or wore towels around their heads and necks when on the river.

At 1730 it was time to make camp again and try out the latest sleeping-sack modifications. A good feed and a comfortable night's sleep were always something to look forward to: getting bitten by thousands of mosquitos was not.

A good night's sleep was had and the sleeping sack changes worked well, although it was hot in the sack and the temperature at night rarely fell below 75°F. It was necessary to wear jeans, socks and a long-sleeved T-shirt whilst in the sack, as the rugged mosquitos of these regions could get their needles through a single layer of even the thickest cotton. Two layers was just beyond their reach. With the increased opening on the facial area I was able to breathe better and sweat a lot less. The mosquito netting was uncomfortable where it touched my face but I would find a way round that later.

It was now a month since I had begun the expedition and it was time for another assessment. I was feeling much the same as the day I started, quite healthy and fit. The mosquitos without a doubt had been the single most serious problem but I hoped I was now close to a solution. Lesser problems were an aching wrist and petty thieving. I made a note that the variety of food could be improved upon. I was getting enough to eat but would prefer a wider menu. Breakfast had focused in on porridge and eggs, and supper would frequently be tinned food and fruit. During the day I would eat bananas or water melon, depending on what was available. Fruits like oranges appealed to me but they were hard to get outside the big towns like Pucallpa. Rice was in abundance in this area so I might include some of that in my diet.

It was scorching hot again today but progress was good. Near Saman I stumbled on a little village, on a bluff at a bend on the river and easy to miss. A small community, with hand-me-down skills in boat-building, they made heavy wooden motor boats about thirty feet long, with thick timbers. Nothing was made streamlined or delicate on the Amazon;

ruggedness was the main criterion. The tools used were very basic, the trained eye being substituted for the ruler.

One of the women of the village specialised in making small cakes and offered me some at fifty soles apiece: they were delicious so I bought a dozen. Nowhere else on the Amazon was I to find anything similar. I was particularly glad I had stopped by because I had estimated it to be a two-egg town but surprisingly was offered three. I bought these and travelled on.

By 1730 it was time to camp but I just could not find a sandbank. Then I spotted a small beach next to a field of crops being tilled by a group of women so I decided to seek permission to make camp. Predictably the women fled as I beached the kayak and soon the men were on the scene, machetes in hand. A big smile, wish them the time of day, tell them I'm on my way to Iquitos and ask permission to stay the night. Yes, no problem, said someone I took to be the foreman. Pointing to a group of huts across the river he said, "You can sleep there." I told him that this would do fine.

I had learned to show people that I had food with me, otherwise they would be unsure whether some of their crops would vanish during the night. Looking at something as small as a kayak, they were unlikely to believe that I was self-sufficient. Producing a few packs of freeze-dried foods, I would say, "Here is my food. Five minutes in hot water and eat." Perhaps I would also show them the oats and eggs and if they still were not happy I would show them the sleeping-sack and mosquito net, saying, "My bed is here also." By now they would be convinced and laughing. "A total system," they would say, "and only this."

Some of my money had got damp and was starting to rot, so as it was a fine morning next day I laid it out on the beach to dry. It was just as well I had checked it because another week or so and it would have been unusable. I took the opportunity to check some of the containers I seldom used to see if any dampness was at work there. Everything seemed in order and I replaced them.

By 1000 the ladies had plucked up courage to come and talk to me. A small group of them, carrying bunches of peanut plants for me, came down to see how I lived. They were all smiling now so I took their photo. I think the smiles of the younger ones said more than good morning. They sat down by my kayak and had a good giggle. "Only this," they would say, "only this."

It was a late take-off today, 1100, and once more the sun was scorching. Glassy calm water and the glare was strong. At 1300 I spotted a small double-decker cargo vessel, the MV *Rosita*, tied up at an unmarked village. It was about a hundred tons and typical of the vessels that plied their trade between Pucallpa and Iquitos. They carried general cargo, surplus crops, goods for local shops and perhaps some drums of fuel. I was to see one or two vessels of this category every day from now on and a friendly chat could often provide useful bits of information.

I mentioned the names of a couple of towns downstream and asked if they were commercial. "Oh yes, they are commercial," I was told "and you will find everything you want there." "Would you like to eat?" one crewman asked, showing me a turtleshell. I did not need asking twice and was soon on board and sitting at the galley table.

My face was burning and they gathered I was thirsty. "Would you like some *refresco*?" the cook asked me. This is a soft drink made with lemon and sugar. "Yes, please," I said as politely as I could. They could not find a mug big enough for what I would need, so they gave me a large bowl of the stuff and stood there laughing as I polished it off in record time. It virtually vaporised as it hit my tongue. Then came the rice and turtle meat. It was delicious. "Where to after Iquitos?" asked one crew member. "Leticia and Manaus," I replied. "But Manaus is like the ocean," he said, not comprehending that a kayak could handle that. "No problem," I replied.

By now most of the young kids from the village had come on board to see me. The crew kept asking questions. How did I get the kayak from Australia to Peru? "By plane," I said. "How much did that cost?" "Four hundred dollars," I said. "And how about your own fare?" "Sixteen hundred dollars." This was something I did not like discussing. These were fantastic amounts of money to local people and setting the impression that I was rich was not wise. About an hour later, after exchanging names and addresses with the captain, I climbed into the kayak.

"You are going to Iquitos then?" said the cook. "Could you take her with you?" He pointed at the only female crew member. (She was the cook's assistant.)

"Oh yes, I could fit her in somewhere," I replied. They all laughed. So by 1400 I was on my way again.

About half an hour downstream, a motorised canoe with two men aboard pulled out and tried to stop me. "What do you want?" I asked. They would not say. One man kept repeating, "Hey mister. Hey, mister." He pulled alongside the kayak and grabbed the front carry-handle. The second man held out his hand, asking for money. I brought the edge of the paddle blade across the back of the first man's hand, he gave a yell and let go. His motor had stalled, so I moved on downstream while he tried to restart it. To stop me again he would almost certainly ram me; it would be the only effective way. I moved into the shallows and loosened the knife from its sheath. My drill was set. I had long since considered the possibility of this happening and I was ready: it would be into their boat with a knife in their throats. It was them or me and there would be no witnesses. I kept paddling without looking back but kept a sharp ear open. Five minutes passed, ten then fifteen and now I could hear the motor. I still did not look back but relied on hearing alone to fix their position. Soon I could see them from the corner of my eye, sixty feet out to the right and slightly behind me. They drew parallel and passed on. It was not them. A similar boat but three different people. I travelled on another ten miles and slept on a sandbank.

Saturday, 11th September was washday and while my shirt and shorts were drying I made a further modification to the sleeping sack. Using some spare cloth, I made a thick rim that would rest on my forehead and keep the hood and mosquito netting clear of my nose and mouth. Apart from being itchy if the netting was too close to my face, the mosquitos could get their needles through to me.

The camp spot was comfortable and I was able to relax and enjoy the morning. Dolphins were rounding up fish nearby and I spent some time trying to get a good action shot of them with my still camera.

My clothes still were not dry so I tried cooking bananas the way the Indians do: they select the green and unripe ones and boil them until the skin splits. The result tasted something like the potato root yuca. I washed it all down with a cup of coffee and then it was time to leave.

The skies had clouded but there were no storms in sight, good conditions for canoeing. I was under way by 1130 and the current proved useful, speeding me along. Just as well, for there were strange areas that were deathly silent today, stretches where no bird sang nor any animal cried. Without actually seeing anything that could be of danger, instinctively I knew not to stop here. It was an eerie feeling, like a warning. A few miles downstream and everything was fine again. Birds sang, fish jumped clear of the water, monkeys chattered and the sense of danger passed.

By evening I was passing the village of San Roque. It looked very tidy from the river with neat green banks and little thatched huts. But it was close to dark so I decided not to visit. A mile or two further on there was a sharp bend in the river and a large sandbank island had formed. It was lovely to find something like that, soft, clean, dry and almost invariably an abundance of driftwood. Although there was a strong smell of rotting vegetation, it was not the stale, foul odour that first comes to mind at these words, but an almost sweetish smell, not unpleasant.

I seldom bothered building sophisticated camps now unless it looked like rain. Typically, I would lay a plastic groundsheet beside the kayak and sleep on top of it. Most of my gear would be stored in the hatches and the paddles secured over these; if anybody tried to steal anything in the night, I would almost certainly hear them. I kept my knife and flashlamp within easy reach and always checked their position before pulling the hood of my sleeping-bag over my head. If there were any thick sticks of hard wood around, I would fashion a club from these and leave it under the edge of the groundsheet. If a storm occurred during the night, I had my drill well practised: out of the sack, jeans and socks off; shorts on, buoyancy vest and poncho on; sleeping sack and clothes folded and put into the hatches; groundsheet folded and strapped to the stern. Then I would sit in the cockpit until the storm passed; with my poncho on and spread over the cockpit area I was virtually waterproof.

The animal world would crank up at dawn with an amazing array of sounds from the jungle. Some were like old car engines being turned over, while others appeared to be laughing. Soon after dawn the parrots would be off to their feeding grounds, flying in pairs high above the river and having a nag as they travelled, their brilliant plumage looking magnificent in the first rays of sunlight.

I was really enjoying the mornings these days, breakfast was porridge, eggs, fruit, followed by a cup of tea and, if I was still around at ten o'clock, a cup of coffee. I would often have a swim while clothes were drying or batteries for my torch being recharged. The mosquitos were usually gone by sun-up so these few hours were the most pleasant time of day. By late morning the sand would be scorching my feet and the sun's intensity was too strong to be comfortable. Also a nasty black biting fly became very active at this time of day. I would not know it had settled on me until I felt its sudden sharp bite and saw a trickle of blood running down the side of my leg. I hated those damned things.

One morning several families came down from the local village to see me. I just didn't want to be bothered with them as everything was so peaceful. One large group sat in a circle around the kayak to watch how I lived, picking things up and passing comments on them. I felt like asking them if I could bring a bundle of friends into their house and watch how they lived. A mean thought but I did like those mornings to myself.

Some days I stuffed things back into the kayak wherever they would fit, overlooking the balance problem. By the end of the week a sluggish kayak would remind me that I must repack completely.

Sundays were interesting days on the river, times for great socialising when even the smallest boats flew the Peruvian flag as they collected church-goers from the smaller villages and took them to the nearest place that had a church. When I stopped at a small unmarked village between Santa Isabel and Tamango, I found a great many boats tied up so I guessed something was going on. There were two soccer matches in progress; one between the girls and the other between the boys. The small store in the village was doing a roaring trade selling beer and buns, and a small mud bakery nearby was going flat out to keep up with demand. After I bought my supplies, most of the village came down to the river to see me off; the football matches stopped and the players lined the banks, plying me with the usual questions; where was I from and where was I going? How did I get my kayak into Peru? Would it sink if a wave hit it? Few understood its abilities and many labelled it 'Gringo's submarine'.

Near Tamango a small cargo boat from Iquitos was loading fish caught from the nearby villages. They had crushed ice on board to keep it fresh for the journey. This obviously was a key fishing spot on the Amazon. I was actually shovelling my way through fish as I paddled along. It was so incredible that I had to film it: few fishermen would have believed the tale. I would row into schools of them. Darting in every direction, they seemed not to know which way to run, they would jump clear of the water, landing on the kayak, even hitting me. Most were small, less than a foot, and known locally as trophy fish. If they had been piranhas I would have been going for a water speed record!

The countryside was full of rice paddies and very small settlements. I knew I would be spotted wherever I settled so figured it best to make my case to the locals. A small group of about six people was standing by one rice paddy. I beached the kayak and walked up. The women fled looking genuinely terrified and down came the men with machetes in hand. So I had to do the bare hands, it's only me stunt again and soon we were on talking terms. They were close to full Indian and one woman appeared to retain all the pure characteristics. After telling the men my intentions they asked if I had a little sugar to spare. Since this would involve unpacking the kayak I told them to call over to my camp in the morning and I would give them some. There was a good bank about a mile downstream and that was where I set up camp.

This last incident rekindled thought about the terror stories of the Amazon. These people lived in small, isolated family settlements often consisting of only one or two huts and clearly felt vulnerable to attacks. But who would attack them and for what? They had nothing. Were terror stories handed down from generation to generation? Or was it just that I was different, with fair hair, a bright yellow buoyancy vest and a strange-looking boat that they certainly would not have seen the likes of before? I did not know, but these people were not joking – they were genuinely terrified.

The mosquitos were dense again but, thanks to sack modification mark four, I had a fair night's sleep. I was up by 0545 and decided to have a change of breakfast menu. It was poached eggs and porridge this morning. Nothing like variety! The rice farmer called and I gave him a quarter kilo of sugar. "Do you want some rice?" he asked. As it happened I did but it was a long way back to his hut and I am sure he had more important things to do, so I declined the offer.

The rice paddies followed a regular pattern: on the inside of a bend on the river where the water slowed down and dropped its load, there would be a sandbank formed by the heavier sediment; beyond this, and connected to it, were mudbanks of finer sediment which were used for growing rice. In the wet season the Amazon would overflow on to these mudbanks; when the river receded it left behind a layer of rich minerals and nutrients which made regular annual cropping possible. The lush green paddy fields were a most attractive sight as I paddled by.

At 1300 I stopped at the small, uncharted mestizo village of Santa Fe. What rules were followed for marking villages on the maps I could never fathom. Sometimes there would be little more than a hut but it would be marked, at other times I would come across a well-settled village of 400 people but there would be no mention of it.

There was a small shop in the village which also served as a bar. Above the bar was a large sign with *'Malvinas'* written across it. The woman who ran the place treated me as if I had the plague, stepping well clear of me wherever I walked. After buying some tinned food and eggs I made my way back to the kayak uncertain of my reception. There was a very small school here, even more basic than the one I had seen at San Luis, but the teacher, or professor as he is termed locally, called me over for a chat, and seemed very friendly; the kids gathered round and a couple even offered to sell me water melons. They brought me two small ones and with a sly grin, asked for 500 soles; a bit above the market price, but I bought them anyway. (Large melons sold for around 500 soles, that is seventy cents US). I asked the teacher if there was anywhere where I could get milk powder and he sent one of the kids to get some; while I was waiting the others showed me their exercise books. Hardly understanding a word of it, I told them I thought their work was very good and this brought a few smiles. After collecting the milk powder, I made a small donation to the school and moved on.

By late afternoon I made camp among the rice paddies close to Flor de Punga. A gentle breeze was blowing which kept mosquitos away. Without the mosquitos the evenings could be lovely, listening to the calls of the birds and animals, a refreshing wash in the river or even a swim, supper by the camp fire and a browse over the maps to see how I was progressing. Few animals came close and only the bats would be continually playing a game of near misses. But when the mosquitos were around it was miserable, trying to eat while getting bitten from every angle, dropping food in the sand at a sharp bite on the back of the hand or almost stabbing myself with a fork while attempting to beat them off. All I thought about then was getting into the sack as quickly as possible.

Profile definitely had an effect on swarm densities. Standing upright would bring the least number of attacks. Bending over or sitting down brought a significant increase and lying down brought the maximum intensity. In this position, their noise was deafening. I think there is an atom of logic to this, as mosquitos are more likely to make successful attacks when their victims are lying down or asleep. Sleeping in the upright position did come to mind but I doubted my abilities in this area. According to most authorities on this region, this was the dry season and there were no mosquitos. I wish sincerely that someone would tell the mosquitos that!

Flor de Punga proved to be a fair-sized town, boasting no less than five shops. A large cargo boat was offloading and long lines of labourers were carrying cases of tinned food, flour, soft drinks and beer up the banks. Even bananas were shipped in, and cattle were being driven ashore. I could not help noticing the hostile faces here, nobody seemed to smile; the dourness did not seem to be aimed at me, but I wondered what had happened here in years gone by to create such inbred bitterness.

The shops had a fair range of goods and since river conditions were pretty stable now I decided to take on some extra cargo. This would reduce the number of stops I was making. Tinned food, oats and milk powder were OK for long-term storage, only eggs, fruit and fish posed problems. I rarely carried more than six eggs at a time; this number would last me three days which was the maximum time I could risk keeping them in such intense heat. I purchased two kilos of oats in hermetically sealed tins, two tins of fish, six eggs, six rolls, a bunch of bananas, a coconut and three envelopes. There was no way I could fit it all into the kayak so I dropped most of the tinned food into the cockpit and strapped the fruit to the deck. I would do some cargo reshuffling further downstream where no one would catch sight of my cameras and binoculars as I shifted everything around.

A small crowd gathered to watch me take off, only one person asked my destination. There were still no smiling faces and I was rather surprised when an old woman in the crowd called out, "*Bon voyage*, Gringo." It was the first friendly comment I had heard there.

Half an hour later I stopped on a bank to relocate cargo. I managed to squeeze most of it into the hatches, except for the fruit and two tins of oats. These got secured to the deck. My gradual accumulation of heavier cargo was beginning to show now and ol' kayak starting to look like a pregnant duck!

Next day I gave ol' kayak a good clean up, especially inside the cockpit which had been particularly attracting the mosquitos. My frying-pan had not been used since I started the trip so that got dumped; the butter or oil needed for frying were too difficult to keep in a kayak. Then I used my saw for the first time to cut a coconut up for a lunchtime snack. I was just enjoying the break when I spotted a sandstorm downstream. Quickly I began my drill: everything into the kayak, paddle secured, poncho on and sit tight. A couple of minutes and it was on me, the fire got scattered in all directions and if I had not been sitting in the kayak, that would have gone rolling too. Soon the winds diminished and the rains came. It is a fairly set pattern and so long as its tell-tale warnings are heeded, the dangers can be avoided. When all had passed, I continued with the packing operation and was under way again by late afternoon.

The town of Requena was pretty large, quite possibly the largest between Pucallpa and Iquitos. There was a fair bit of timber milling going on and from the river it all looked rather tidy. I was delighted to find a stock of insect spray in one of the stores. A storm blew up as I was about to leave so I put my poncho on and sat it out for an hour. It seemed a regular daily happening in these parts.

One significant difference I noted in this area was a definite decrease in the number of sandbanks and an increase in the number of mudbanks. Good news for the rice growers but not for the camper. This pattern is not unexpected as the further downstream one gets, the finer the sediment carried along. However, there are some very large tributaries feeding the Amazon along its length so some of them may bring in more coarse sand.

I carried on canoeing till 1800 but failed to locate a suitable bank so it looked like another night by the rice paddies. Unfortunately, there were some dwellings nearby and it was a bit too dark to go knocking on doors. The chances of being welcomed with a machete were fairly high. I turned in and hoped for a good night's sleep. The mosquitos were on vacation.

At 2230 I was woken up by two clumsy drunks wanting to know what I was doing there. I personally believed they had spotted me when I had first arrived but had been drinking up some courage to come and investigate under cover of darkness. One kept striking matches trying to get a better view of the kayak. I put the flashlamp on it and explained my being there. Both were terribly drunk and kept repeating the same questions and tripping over the kayak. I have never had much skill in communicating with drunks and tonight was no exception. After half an hour, they were satisfied and wandered off, taking their now empty spirit bottle with them.

By 0530 it started to rain, so I packed and got under way. It was 0800 before I located a reasonable bank to stop for breakfast and my stomach was rumbling for my morning porridge. A couple of motor canoes pulled close to see what I was up to but I made out I hadn't seen them. I just wanted to eat breakfast. There was no time for tourist parties this morning. Some lumberjacks came down from the forest loaded with sarcasm, but I just didn't have time for them either.

More steady rain in the afternoon. An aluminium motor boat pulled alongside trying to attract my attention. One man was wearing a Texan-style hat and what appeared to be a Texan-style belt buckle. The other man was attempting to wring out a pair of dark blue trousers and show them to me. They cut the engine and drifted closer. Now I got the picture. They were police and that was not a Texan belt buckle but a pair of handcuffs. The other man was merely trying to show me his uniform was soaking wet from the storms, which was why he was not wearing it. He spoke good English and asked who I was, explaining that I had been spotted doing some cooking along the bank and locals were suspicious.

I showed him my identification and he took notes. He was a decent bloke and I rather liked his approach: there was no aggression attached to it. He said at first he thought I might be attached to Jacques Cousteau, whose ship had recently sailed down the Amazon. I told him a little about my trip and he told me of his home town, Arequipa. He also explained the significance of the poles stuck on the bank by the Indians. Apparently they were a way of laying claim to a piece of land. I asked him to write me a note stating that I had indeed been in the area. This he did, we then shook hands and parted company.

With the exception of the checkpoint at Colonia Penal del Sepa, this was the first time I had met police on the river; I had almost forgotten they existed. Most of the small towns and villages in effect police their own regions. One or two senior members of the village will be responsible for checking and reporting any unusual activity along the river, such as a stolen boat or stolen cargo passing through the area.

A few days later I was caught sitting at my fire by a sudden storm. By the time I had everything packed and the poncho on, I was already soaked. Things eased towards midnight and I fought to keep the fire going because a blaze invariably helps morale when you are miserable and wet. At midnight I tried to lie down but the rains returned and saturated the place once more, so the night was spent either sitting in the cockpit or struggling with the fire. A most uncomfortable night with probably no more than an hour's sleep.

Getting caught offguard like that pressured me into modifying my equipment. I decided to have a rapidly erectable cover for the camp. Bivvys took too long to erect and at the end of a day's canoeing I could not always justify the effort. Since I no longer needed the space blanket for sleeping, this would do as a cover. It was waterproof, fairly large (six feet by four feet six) and had eyelets at each corner. One side could be secured to the deck of the kayak and the other to a bank or to a couple of poles stuck in the ground. With ropes already tied to the corners, it would only need a minute or two to get it in position. It would also be more comfortable to sit under during long storms than in the cockpit.

The morning remained overcast and getting things dry was difficult. The sleeping-sack was still damp at 1100 but I decided to move on, hoping to dry it off by the camp fire tonight. I was on my way by 1130 but had great difficulty in keeping my eyes open. By mid-afternoon the glare of the sun combined with lack of sleep proved too much for me and I had to pull off the river. With my hat pulled over my eyes and feet up on the foredeck, I dozed off. Just a fifteen-minute cat-nap but it helped. Another couple of hours' canoeing and I reached the junction of the Ucayali and Marañon rivers. This is the point where the river now takes on the name of the Amazon. Only Brazil disagrees on this point, referring to the river as the Solimões up to Manaus and the Amazon thereafter.

Delightfully, there was a large sandbank opposite the Marañon's entry point which meant that there was a lot of heavier sediment being fed in from the tributary. So I would not have to spend the remainder of the trip camping on the finer silted mudbanks. But I was worried by the amount of trees and flotsam also coming down the Marañon. Huge menacing-looking logs bulldozed their way along, some were off-cuts from timber mills, others were sections of trees that had fallen or been dragged into the river. These would be dangerous enough for day canoeing, let alone the night.

Rain was a strong possibility again tonight and so I erected the space blanket over my camp, then I sprayed the cockpit with insect repellent and began to collect wood, always being extremely careful to check for snakes. Not that these sand-banks and islands were ideal spots for them, as most were less than two metres above the river and so recently formed from deposits left by the last flood that almost nothing grew on them. With no rocks to hide behind, no grass or trees to camouflage themselves in, snakes would be easy prey for hawks and eagles. Snakes might, however, float downstream on a pile of driftwood. I had seen frogs get deposited on sandbanks this way, so I still checked carefully. Crocodiles fortunately were not keen on these low sandbanks. In fact the only creatures that could make use of them were a type of gull that, for reasons best known to itself, laid its eggs on the open patches of sand. These would do no more than create a noisy fuss, swooping low over me as I approached their eggs.

A lovely night's sleep and 21st September dawned on a beautiful day. After a good night's rest to awake gently at the break of dawn is a wonderful experience; I lay there for half an hour without moving, just watching the sky get bluer and bluer, listening to the birds gently break the silence with their morning song.

The second billy can purchased in Contamana proved its worth as I could make tea or coffee in it at the same time as my eggs were cooking in the first one. It was a very solid, rugged metal alloy pot, ideal for this environment. The flimsy gear sold in camping stores might suit neat little primus stoves but most would incinerate on the fires I made.

As I paddled through the shallows to cool my feet, I noticed schools of tiny fish trying to nibble my toes. They were only an inch long and did nothing more than cause a tingling sensation. I thought about piranhas, but as the whole river was teeming with wildlife, why should they be interested in me? They might be dangerous in the creeks and shallow pools where competition for food was fierce, but surely not here.

There was no timetable to keep, no rush to get to work, and if I wanted to do nothing all day but have my feet nibbled by fish that might not be baby piranhas, there would be no problem. The rat race was far from my mind now, and I could not give a damn about it.

The river was getting noticeably wider now, about two miles, and the current stronger; I estimated it to be around three to four knots. The debris certainly required extra attention today; worst of all were the semi-submerged logs. Sometimes the first I would know of them was a heavy thump as they impacted the kayak. Fibreglass was wonderful stuff but it could not take too much of that.

By mid-afternoon dark clouds were looming over the horizon and lightning flashing almost continuously. An hour passed and the storm still had not reached me. Then bolts of lightning flashed close by and the thunder hammered its way up the Amazon. There was a good bank visible just a couple of miles on, but could I make it? Adverse winds were giving me a hard time now and chop was picking up. If I stopped here till the storm passed, I would have to canoe on towards the bank in the dark amidst the logs and debris. First splashes of rain were hitting me now but the bank was getting closer. Just on 1730 the storm unleashed its fury but I had made it up on to the bank, poncho on and was sitting in the cockpit, my back to the storm.

It was 2000 before it passed and the wood I managed to gather was well saturated with no special desire to burn. Even with my boy-scout experience, it took almost an hour to start looking like a fire. A large fallen tree-trunk conveniently made one wall of my camp. I secured one side of the space blanket to it and the other end to the top of the kayak, so that the rain water would run off down a thirty-degree slope rather than form a huge sagging pool in the centre. It was fish for supper again, followed by chocolate milk and bed at 2200.

The mist cleared soon after dawn and another fine day was in the making. How easy it was to find wood once it was light. I must almost have been tripping over the stuff. After my now very standard breakfast of porridge and eggs, a fishing boat pulled on to the bank and asked to borrow the fire. This was not unusual for fishermen were often out long before dawn and liked to cook a few of their catch for breakfast before returning home. The fish had been sorted into species and size, the variety was quite phenomenal. One of the fishermen recited the names for me including paitsche, trophy and pirarucu – the world's largest freshwater fish capable of outweighing a man and almost reaching six feet in length – but they didn't offer me any. Fishermen were invariably a rowdy bunch but cheerful and friendly.

I was on my way by 0915 and a couple of miles downstream spotted a launch loading melons. They seem to grow almost wild in this region. "How much for a melon?" I asked. Without saying a word, I was thrown one. A real bargain, I thought, and paddled on.

Tamshiyaco was the last town of any size before Iquitos and by midday I was there. There was a floating restaurant at the foot of the town and I got permission to pull the kayak aboard. It seemed fairly safe there, so I climbed the steps into town and made a few purchases. Large packs of thick biscuits were for sale and since I rarely got bread on the river, these would do for a substitute. I also refilled my eggbox and got some more tinned food. The more I could get here, the less time I would need to spend in Iquitos. I had never actually been to Iquitos but I knew that the kayak could not be safely left on its own for too long in a busy town: the chances of robbery were far less in a small close-knit community.

The kayak was still in one piece when I returned so I figured I could take a meal at the restaurant to say thank you. It had a big menu: rice and turtle meat, or turtle meat, rice and beans. I chose the latter. The meal was well cooked and steaming hot so I hoped it would not give me too many stomach problems. I avoided the drinks, as I knew they were made from untreated Amazon water with flavouring. It never ceased to amaze me how every village and town, large or small, sold stomach powders, tablets and medicines to the local inhabitants but no one told them to boil the river water before drinking it. An unhealthy race cannot be an advantage to any nation. "Will it rain?" I asked the locals, purely to make conversation. A brief look at the sky and they said, "Definitely it will rain." Not really paying much attention to the answer, I climbed into the kayak and waved farewell. Less than half a mile downstream, the heavens opened and I was soaked. There were no suitable banks to run to so I just kept going. The chop was not high but visibility was down to a few feet. A sudden blast from a ship's horn made me get into higher gear rather sharply. It was a 1000-ton cargo boat and it nearly caught me side on.

By mid-afternoon the weather was fine and I was steaming dry as I paddled on. Ideally, I wanted to get as close to Iquitos as possible so I could reach the town by early next morning. Most of the shops and businesses would close down about midday and would not open again until late afternoon. Hanging around that long did not appeal to me. I continued canoeing till 1730 and then made camp. I estimated I was about seven miles or an hour's paddling from Iquitos.

I was becoming more skilled at organising my camps now. Each night I dragged the kayak ashore, filled water containers so that the sediment had time to settle out, washed in the river, gathered wood and lit a fire. All pots and containers, food and equipment removed from the kayak were always laid in neat rows along its side or in the cockpit and as I finished with each item, it would be replaced in the hatches. Only the knife and flashlamp would be left out at night and these had fixed positions. A good disciplined approach like this kept losses down virtually to zero. Organisation also enabled me to get packed and away quickly each morning.

At 0900 I was on my way in light drizzle. By 0930 the heavens opened and I was soaked but there was no point in stopping now. Visibility was poor so I hugged the banks where possible, as shipping was getting very busy near the town. There was some confused water as I crossed the harbour but the visibility improved. By 1030 I was there and the sun shining as if to mock my efforts through the storm.

Now came the problem of finding a place to leave the kayak for a while: to the left Iquitos appeared to be a waterside slum and the far right was the dock area and naval base – too far from the central shopping areas to suit me. Along the central river front were a few small docking facilities, floating repair and boat sheds, one of which looked respectable and not too busy.

"Can I leave my kayak here for a couple of hours," I asked, "while I do some shopping?"

I got some strange looks but they agreed. The place belonged to a Canadian missionary. That sounded safe enough to me so I hauled the kayak up aboard and went in to the town.

The first stop was the bank to try again for some Brazilian cruzeiros. Still wearing my buoyancy vest and dripping wet, I got the strangest looks as I entered the bank. "No cruzeiros," I was told so I would have to try at the Brazilian border. Next stop was the post office but for reasons best known to themselves it was closed for the day. I had yet to pass a letter over a post office counter on this trip. No insect spray available so I would have to use my present can carefully. Fortunately, food was no problem and in great variety. I stocked up with all I needed and also replaced my broken flip-flops and disposable gas lighter.

At 1300 I returned to the boat shed and found the owners there, Mr and Mrs Ronald Coles of the United Pentecost Church. I told them a little about my trip and asked Mrs Coles if she would post my letters for me, by now soaking wet. Mrs Coles agreed and waited to see me off. She thought I was very brave. It was nice to get such compliments but the expedition was still more of a burning ambition in my mind than any act of bravery.

I passed four old war ships tied up at the naval dockyard; how incredible to find such things 2400 miles up the Amazon. A mile or two downstream there was a good bank so I pulled off the river to dry my clothes. Just one hour under the intense sun and they were beautifully dry. I put them on again and what a boost to morale that was. Clean and dry, I felt fit for anything. A quick check of the charts and it was back with the action. Current was still strong and progress was good.

Friday, 24th September was overcast but dry. There had been a few showers in the night but nothing heavy. Being a Friday, I took my Maloprin tablet and made a note of it in the log. I hate to think how many times I must have been bitten by malaria carrying mosquitos but the tablets seem to be rendering them harmless.

The charts I had of this area were a vast improvement, they were so much more accurate that I presumed that they were drawn from surveys made somewhere between the wet and dry seasons. This made plotting my course and planning the day much easier. Most prominent features were marked; also small islands and banks that would not have been visible in the wet season. A few of the narrower channels marked were no longer in existence as water levels were insufficient to feed them. The scale of these charts was approximately one nautical mile to a centimetre, compared to approximately nine nautical miles (or eighteen kilometres) to a centimetre on maps up to Iquitos. I kept the chart strapped to the deck in front of me: it was good to know exactly where I was. Progress was excellent today and I watched the miles tick by at an average speed around six knots.

At midday a motor launch carrying three businessmen pulled alongside and handed me a nice cold Coke, a tin of sausages and a pack of biscuits. All three then shook hands, wished me a *bon voyage* and roared off again. People could be fantastic at times. I let the kayak drift in midstream while I enjoyed the free lunch. There was no point in going into the bank. The river was about two miles wide here and that would be wasted energy. The water was calm and it was not necessary to get stomach ulcers trying to keep the kayak stable and eat at the same time.

By evening, I had checked my charts and estimated that I had covered thirty-five nautical miles that day which is approximately forty statute miles.

On 25th September I reached the very small settlement of San Salvador, only twenty homes but a friendly bunch of people. It was definitely no more than a two-egg town and that was all I got. I was also handed a water melon and no money would be accepted. One lady of the village told me a gringo boat had passed through yesterday, it had a motor but she did not know how many gringos were on it. I had not heard anybody from the Explorers' Club mention any expeditions to this area and I could not help wondering who it was.

I stopped a mile further on from the village to eat the water melon. Large ones would do for two snacks, small ones around a kilo, only one snack. The water was seething with fish and once again I actually had to shovel my way through water frothing and bubbling with their activity. They were so closely packed their fins must have been touching. There was something about this spot they liked. It would have been easy to slap the paddle hard on the surface and kill a few for supper but I had second thoughts about it; I had not wanted for food this far into the trip and I might be upsetting somebody by fishing in their area.

I paddled on until almost 1700 and made camp on an island approximately ten nautical miles before Pebas. These lens-shaped islands were everywhere now and most of them had good camp spots; they were also uninhabited so I could remain undetected. I did not have to explain my presence to anyone and nobody bothered me.

I was enjoying being alone more and more. I often thought how marvellous it would be to travel on like this for ever. I had seen some beautiful places on the trip and it was at times like these that I felt like saying, "Just leave me here in a world free from politics." It was so peaceful.

On Sunday, 26th September I was up at 0430, got the fire going and washed my polo neck and jeans. It was a fine but hazy day and winds were picking up – good for drying clothes, but seldom of any use to the canoeist. Even on exceptionally rare occasions when winds were favourable, the extra chop they created reduced efficiency.

It was take off at 0900 and soon I was soaked with spray from waves breaking over the bow. At 1000 a large white launch with what appeared to be a dragon's head on its bow passed me and sounded its horn. Now the picture fitted. This is the gringo launch I have been told about and only Jacques Cousteau would have anything as sophisticated as that on the Amazon. At 1200 I reached Pebas and bought a few more provisions at a floating store. Just across the river the Cousteau Society's boat, *Calypso*, had anchored so I paid them a visit.

The crew was a mixed bunch of scientists, technicians, divers and pilots. There were about twenty-five in all and they were doing an environmental study of the Amazon area. World concern over the logging operations and other environmental problems had prompted the expedition. They certainly had a wide range of equipment for the job; apart from the laboratory and sophisticated navigation equipment, there was also a seaplane, a helicopter, hovercraft and inflatable runabouts. It was almost embarrassing to say that I was on an expedition with ol' kayak and a plastic compass. After a coffee and an interesting chat with the crew, I got the captain to witness my presence there and pushed on. An array of cameras shot my departure making me feel like a movie star as I pulled away.

At 1600 I had clocked up thirty-five nautical miles and that would do for today. I camped on the Isla Pixana and for supper tried my hand at rice pudding. I had not a clue how it was made so it was a matter for trial and error.

First I boiled the rice for half an hour and then added a couple of large spoonfuls of sugar and milk powder, stirred well and it was ready. It did not taste too bad, a bit rubbery, but then it was filling and wide tolerances are always allowed for camping food.

Monday, 27th September looked a good day for canoeing. There was no wind and light cloud kept the sun from being too intense. The river was running rapidly at this point, approximately five knots, which was good news to me. However, a considerable increase in flotsam, especially large logs, was not.

At 1700 I met the *Calypso* again and was invited to come aboard for supper as soon as they had secured an anchorage. But with the soft river bed and strong currents, this took more time than anticipated and by 1800 it was getting too dark and dangerous for me to follow them, so I pulled over to a large island, Isla Poca Playa, and made camp. It was another rice pudding for supper. Next day our timing was better. I paddled a couple of miles upstream to where the *Calypso* was anchored, and arrived just as salad and spaghetti were being served for lunch.

Off again at 1200 and progress was good. At 1400 I passed the leper colony at San Pablo and by 1630 I reached San Juan as a storm broke. I seemed to have more than enough Peruvian money left and since the range of goods had increased in this region, I decided to spoil myself with a few luxuries as I approached the border. Big mouth-watering tins of sliced peaches and fruit cocktail were on sale. I could not resist them. I also took the opportunity to top up with other supplies.

There were two checkpoints to go through at Chimbote: the first was military and the second the civil police. The latter wanted to know why I had not got my passport exit stamp in Iquitos. I explained that I wasn't aware that I should have cleared immigration there. In any case, I would have been required to state which day I would be crossing the border – not very easy to predict in a kayak. The official seemed reasonably happy with that answer and told me to get my passport stamped at Alegria before crossing the border.

Later that afternoon a large wooden motor boat passed, full of people who seemed fascinated by my kayak. One man held up a melon, then dropped it in the river for me to pick up. The only problem was spotting it, as it only just floated, scarcely showing above the surface. Light was beginning to fade and this, combined with the ripples on the water, made the melon impossible to spot. The motor boat stopped and I went over to thank them anyway. They insisted that I take a couple of the largest melons they had, in fact, they were so large I could barely get them into the cockpit.

There was a complete family here from grandchildren right up to grandparents and they were all excited to know about my trip. A couple of young ladies seemed especially interested and asked me why I did not stop off at their village for the night. I told them I would be travelling on for a while yet but they still insisted. "It is almost dark now," said one. "And it looks like rain," said another. I thanked them for the kindness and paddled on.

Now I did have to get my finger out. It was very close to dark, the current was running strongly and I had at least five miles to go. According to my chart, the main flow was around the northern channel of the island so I predicted a beach or bank would occur at the far end. By the time I actually reached the island it was almost dark and something was wrong. No matter how I tried I could not keep course for the main channel. I was being dragged across the river to the southern side. I estimated the current to be around ten knots and there was very little point in doing battle with it. It was dark and dead trees were looming up everywhere. I was also considering dumping the melons as they totally restricted any movement in the cockpit and they were not exactly lightweight. I continued to follow the current stream, straining my eyes to spot the logs and trees sticking up from the river bed like deathtraps. Rushing water was invariably the first indication that a trunk was impeding the flow of water. Once a canoe is jammed under a trunk or branch with a strong current flowing against it, the chances of retrieving it are virtually zero. And if anybody is in it at the time, their chances are about the same.

Eventually the water slowed and I moved towards the south bank of the island. I realised that the northern channel had silted up and nearly all the flow was now being redirected through the southern channel. My chart was three years old and already out of date. Later I was to find that even one-month-old maps were obsolete. The Amazon had a mind of its own and would switch channels at will. Even the *Calypso*, with all its modern navigation equipment, never sailed at night.

The mosquitos had made a big comeback and gave me a hard time as I probed through the shallows looking for a bank. At the downstream end of the island was a fair-sized sandpatch and conveniently, a six-foot-deep channel cut through its centre. This was probably formed at the end of the last wet season. I dragged the kayak into the channel and used one of its banks as a fixing point for the camp cover. It was rice pudding again followed by water melon for supper and bed by 2100.

At 0400 the channel wall fell in on me, but it was only sand so I wriggled free and got back to sleep until a heavy downpour turned my dry channel into a river, so it was storm drill time. My sleeping sack plus a few kilos of sand got piled into the hatches and wet sand stuck all over me. I sat it out for a couple of hours but the rains were here to stay. There was hardly any wood about and lighting a fire didn't justify the effort. So it was a big change for breakfast today – a tin of sardines, a tin of mixed fruit and the best part of a water melon.

By 1200 I was tired of waiting and pushed off. Almost instantly the rain stopped and within a few minutes a ray of sunshine was creeping through. I averaged around six knots for most of the afternoon and by 1700 was within five miles of Alegria, the last Peruvian control point on the river. This was to be my last camp in Peru and I made it on the Isla St Helena. After a well-needed clean up and a supper of sardines, rice pudding and chocolate milk, I relaxed by the fire and thought over the trip so far. Most of the self-proclaimed experts on the region had long since been proven wrong and the majority of documentaries I had seen on the Amazon were little more than a farce. Documentaries are an effective way of educating people but those I had seen of this area had failed miserably. Ask almost any man or woman if they would swim in the Amazon for a million dollars and they would say, "No way." The spiced-up documentaries had long since warned them of that. The same would apply if you asked them to spend a week camping on the banks of the Amazon without a firearm. I had washed in the Amazon each day and frequently swum in it. I still had ten fingers and ten toes, and the Indians had not speared me to death.

So how did I feel about the trip so far? In a word: fantastic. People had been great. Before me lay 2000 more miles of the Amazon. The river would be wider from now on, expanding from two miles at the Brazilian border until it gradually reached 125 miles across at its mouth. Ahead lay areas where some of its titanic forces were said to be unleashed. A few I had seen already; others I had only heard of.

11   ACROSS THE BORDER

On Friday, 1st October I was up before the sun. The skies were clear and a hot day predictable. I brought my washing up to date. I would be crossing the border today and I might have to convince some official that I was a respectable gentleman.

At 1300 I reached the Alegria control point. There was a settlement here and a large crowd gathered round to see the kayak as my passport was stamped. A young man who spoke English walked along with me asking about the trip. As we passed a group of teenage girls, one smiled and told her friend she thought I was nice. The young man caught the remark and in language that left nothing to the imagination told me that if I stayed the night, she was mine. The crowd roared with laughter as I politely declined the offer in case it upset my schedule.

At 1600 I reached the border between Peru and Brazil. Across the river on the northern bank is another border between Brazil and Colombia. My plan now was to find somewhere safe for the kayak while I got the immigration and money-changing problems sorted out. I crossed the river to Tabatinga and tried to find somewhere suitable to tie up along the bank but there was nothing available. I spotted a boatshed owned by the Brazilian army and asked the soldier on duty if I could stay there. He just shrugged his shoulders. However, one of his superiors came down to the edge of the river and saw me off.

It was getting close to dark now so I either had to find a shed in the next few minutes or move clear of the town and make camp for the night. About half a mile further upstream I spotted a now familiar boat – the *Calypso* was in port. Jacques Cousteau was away on business, so I asked Mme Cousteau for permission to stay on board until I got my immigration problems sorted out. My kayak would certainly be safe here. A hammock on deck would have been a luxury to me, but Mme Cousteau arranged a cabin for me and I felt quite spoiled.

I had my first real shower since the trip started and generally tidied myself up. This was the first time I had seen myself in a full-length mirror for nearly two months and I was rather surprised how ribby I looked. I must have lost about five kilos, nearly a stone. At 1900 I joined the crew for a lovely roast beef dinner, followed by fruit salad. I even had a small glass of wine, one of my 'no no's' for the trip when I'm in charge of the kayak.

I found it difficult to sleep. It was just too comfortable for me. I eventually dozed off but slept very lightly.

On Saturday, 2nd October I handed over my letters of introduction at Immigration and got a ninety-day-stamp in my passport. The *Calypso* crew told me I'd get the best exchange rate for cruzeiros at Leticia, a cab-ride across the Colombian border. With a population of 22,000, Leticia was a fairly large town and I took the opportunity to browse through the shops. My space-blanket cover had started to tear at the corners and the poncho was looking the worse for wear. Plastic ponchos were on sale at the marinas and I found a suitable one. Finding a lightweight cover to replace the space blanket proved more difficult. Plenty of heavy-duty tarpaulins in town but both weight and bulk were prohibitive. Insect spray was available and this was really good news.

By now it was lunchtime and I could not resist the smell of beefsteaks being cooked at a nearby restaurant. It was time to spoil myself again for a full hour. I had so often thought of good food on the trip. I enjoyed the food I made, especially the morning porridge, but thoughts of sitting down in luxurious restaurants with long menus were always appealing.

Mme Cousteau allowed me another night on board *Calypso* and made sure I got an extra helping of chocolate pudding at supper. She also presented me with two Cousteau Society T-shirts. I guess she figured mine looked a bit grotty.

While the kayak was up on deck, I was able to examine its under parts. The gel-coat had started to wear thin at the bow and near the cockpit through being dragged fully loaded up on to sandbanks each night. It did not look too serious at this stage but it was worth keeping an eye on.

I enjoyed talking to the crew, all specialists in their own fields. One suggested that vitamin B1 gives off an odour imperceptible to humans but which repels mosquitos, another thought I should try solving my problem by eating garlic. I had managed to find some packets of garlic seasoning in town and thought in future I would try this on my breakfast eggs. There must be some truth in the idea that the foods you eat produce skin odours which attract or repel mosquitos. In India many years ago I can remember being continuously bitten, while Indians in the same room had no such problems.

When the subject of robbers and bandits was brought up, Mme Cousteau had the last word. "You are past all the bad areas now," she said, giving special mention to Iquitos and Leticia. Most, including myself, were inclined to agree. But the test would come in the next two months.

At 0830 on 3rd October, I was under way. The weather was fine, the river calm and progress good. I had a few language adjustments to make now and my English/Portuguese Diction-ary got a browse over from time to time.

My first impressions of Brazil were not good. People did not appear to be as friendly as in Peru and most villages bristled with guns. The lack of friendliness may, in part, have been due to the width of the river. People on the opposite bank were like those of another country; there seemed very little contact between them.

In early afternoon I pulled up at a small village and tried for a melon and some eggs. One man saw me coming and im-mediately began shooting at tin cans with his revolver. I am not impressed by guns, nor by the people that hide behind them. So I walked past him and entered the village store. He was not satisfied with this so he came in, put his gun on the table and started drinking. I still totally ignored him and bought my supplies. As I was leaving, he filled his glass and offered it to me. It was his last desperate attempt to get attention. I declined his offer, telling him that I did not drink and walked off. I had spoiled his day and was glad.

Conditions remained good and by evening I had reached Ilha do Ourique and predictably found a sandbank there. The only thing I had not predicted was a settlement at the same place. There was none marked on my chart. The islands were now much bigger, many above maximum flood level become settlements. I carried on to the downstream peak of the island

and found a hard mudbank there. It was too close to the town to light fires, so it was a sardines and biscuits supper.

That night I made the mistake of accidentally inhaling my mosquito repellent as I struggled to reapply it while sitting out a storm. It made me feel more ill than it ever did the mosquitos, but by the next evening I had managed thirty-seven nautical miles and pulled into a large beach with a solitary hut on it. A man and two youths stood about a hundred yards away, so I walked towards them to explain my presence. But they ran off. I didn't know what to think. Here was I, empty-handed, walking towards a grown man and two teenage youths and they ran for their lives. I walked back to the kayak and ate some melon. All three were now standing about 200 yards from me, watching. I waved repeatedly and beckoned them over, and gingerly they walked forward, hesitating at irregular intervals and looking very worried. I gave them a few biscuits each and explained in halting Portuguese that I was on my way to Manaus and would be spending the night here. To the last part, the man just shook his head and said, "No." It didn't matter what I said, his answer was invariably a nervous, "No." He was about twenty-five to thirty, possibly an elder brother of the others, but I really couldn't respect him as a man. It was no use staying here with such a hopeless relationship, so I paddled on for another mile or so and made camp.

By now there were a few minor repairs to be done, such as stitching up the fraying edge of my space blanket and rejoining the fibreglass paddle, which had started to loosen at its joint. The canopy had not lived up to expectations so I burnt the framework, as it was a waste of cargo space.

The next afternoon I reached Santa Rita do Weil and was very surprised to find a rice shortage. There had been such an abundance of it in Peru I had not bothered keeping much in reserve. However, tinned food and eggs were readily available so I stocked up. There is a large sandbank island just half a mile from the town where I camped for the night. I checked my charts and noticed that none of the shallow areas or banks near the town were charted so they must have occurred in the last year or two. It is seldom more than a point of interest and a bit of extra canoeing to me, but to a large cargo vessel the Amazon must be a navigational nightmare. If the present trend at Santa

Rita continues, I believe that that town will soon be left at least half a mile inland.

São Paulo de Olivenca, a large commercial centre, was the next town down river. Here some local youths let their mouths run away with them in simple and sarcastic observations about the gringo's submarine. This sort of thing can get very monotonous. A couple of dugouts tried to race me, which I enjoyed. Theoretically, with two or three men in a canoe, they should have been able to beat me, and after all they have had a lifetime of experience in canoes. Certainly they thought it was going to be a push-over.

Typically, they pulled alongside, still loaded with sarcasm and asked where I was heading. When I mentioned somewhere hundreds of miles down the river, they began to taunt and jeer. Without making it noticeable, I gradually increased the pressure on my paddle so they now had to paddle fairly hard to keep up. The laughing gave way to more serious questions, like how much does my canoe cost? I answered as if unconcerned. By now their panting was noticeable; they had no spare wind for sarcasm. Soon they dropped back; in desperation they tried to distract me by asking if I wanted to buy fish or fruit. I politely answered in the negative without looking back. Now came silence as they dropped out of the race and drifted. I could afford myself a glance back: they looked a sorry lot. It was a very satisfying way to beat mouthaches. The technology and efficiency of modern-day canoes and equipment is something they don't begin to understand, and it only ever takes two-thirds of my maximum speed to keep them going flat out.

Speaking of speed, it was now time to raise my daily rate and keep a check on the mileage in order to complete my expedition in the dry season. Luckily this was now easier to do as I had more detailed charts for this section. But the river was very much wider now and dropping in to odd villages for a couple of eggs was out: zig-zagging across a river this wide wasted a lot of time and energy, therefore stop-offs had to be planned more carefully. Since departing from Leticia, I had decided on a minimum target of thirty nautical miles per day (approximately thirty-four statute miles) or 210 nautical miles a week (approximately 240 statute miles) which should enable me to reach my destination, Cape Maguari, around early December at the end of the dry season. Drifting too far from that schedule could leave me in trouble.

On 8th October I reached Amataura and was surprised at its size. The town itself is a contrast – old cathedral-like structures at the centre, as if from a bygone age, surrounded by modern buildings. There were five stores along the waterfront and the range of goods was impressive. I spent about 1500 cruzeiros here while most of the stores' customers stood in silence, not sure what to make of me. Store owners seem to have a big problem with mental arithmetic throughout the entire Amazon region. Life is rather slow in these parts of the world and speed and accuracy are strange words. I frequently had to add the bills up for them. If not, they invariably made a mistake, in over half the cases undercharging rather than overcharging.

Wind and white caps were the weather pattern now and I was glad to make an island camp spot as light faded.

Around midnight strange voices woke me up. About one mile diagonally across the river some kind of ceremony was taking place. A man appeared to be preaching to a group of people who responded intermittently. Suddenly, a woman let out a blood-curdling scream, but the voice of the man I had taken to be the preacher still carried on amid her hysterical shrieking. After listening for a few minutes, I was convinced it was a voodoo ceremony. They are not uncommon in Brazil but as it had nothing to do with me, I went back to sleep.

Saturday, 9th October started dry with light winds. It is now two months since I set out and the gloomy predictions of the most optimistic of my well-wishers and advisers have not been fulfilled. I am still alive. More than that, I am in good health. Food variety has improved slightly and such minor problems as an aching wrist have gone.

By early afternoon a heavy storm was visible on the horizon but it appeared not to be coming upstream. However within five minutes strong winds were blowing and the chop picking up. I was about a mile out and the paddle was almost being torn from my hands. I kept the nose into the wind and rollers while ferry-gliding back to the shore. By the time I got there, the storm had arrived and unleashed its fury.

I was angry with myself for not knowing better. At the first sign of that storm I should have moved towards the bank instead of staying in midstream hoping it would pass over. As usual, it did not last long, just a few of nature's forces rebalancing themselves. So long as I am lucky enough not to get hit by a bolt of lightning I actually enjoy storms: there is nowhere to run for protection so I might just as well sit in the kayak with my poncho on and wait till it passes.

Within an hour things were looking better and I pushed off again. Fifteen minutes later, passing the north-eastern tip of Ilha Pupona, I got a few more nasty moments. Two channels of the river, both running around five knots, meet violently at this point and, to make things worse, the river was still very disturbed from the storm, with large rollers coming upstream. The net result was confused and dangerous water. It was eyes in every direction, as mountains of water spiked up from every angle. These conditions are very unforgiving and you use up twice the normal amount of energy and concentration to tackle them.

During the next two days the winds turned westerly which is so totally alien to the Amazon I couldn't help wondering if it boded ill. The Amazon exists because easterly winds pick up moisture which they drop again before the Andes. These westerlies really puzzled me.

I was getting fed up with answering the same questions – "Where are you going?" "Where have you come from?" – over and over again, so in big capitals I scrawled CUZCO–IQUITOS–LETICIA–MANAUS–BELÉM along the side of ol' kayak in black marker pen. Belém was not my intended final destination, but it's the best known place near to it. To put Cabo Maguari would have invited more questions than it answered. I also added the estimated distance – 4000 miles. What purpose this would serve was doubtful. Everybody on the Amazon talks in number of hours or days between places; for obvious reasons kilometres or miles have very little significance. This system is possibly inherited from the Indians. Canoes are estimated to take three times as long as motor boats, so when discussing distances the type of boat has to be specified. The only variation to this system was in the remoter areas of Peru. Some people would talk of the number of bends you had to pass through to reach a certain destination. The problem here was knowing what counted as a bend to the locals. Did it have to be something close to a U-bend or did a gentle curve qualify?

Generally speaking, discussing distances on the river is nothing more than a bit of idle chat, an excuse to introduce yourself to an area. There were instances where I was given from one to five hours for the same destination. If I really needed an accurate assessment of distance to a certain place, the best way was to ask a group of people and, regardless of what the first one told me, to sound very sceptical. This would invariably lead to heated discussion among the group, each one of whom claimed to know best. By the time the argument finished, I would have gained a fairly realistic figure.

Some of my equipment was beginning to deteriorate and it looked as if repairs would have to be carried out soon. My spray cover was rotting from being under the scorching sun for too long, the rubber backing was peeling off leaving only the nylon cloth. Apart from weakening it, this meant it was no longer waterproof. Also, the front carry-handle rope was starting to fray.

I reached a small commercial town at the junction of the river Jutai and spent almost an hour buying supplies at a couple of floating stores. The Jutai is much clearer than the Amazon and there is some beautiful scenery upstream. A narrower meandering river with rich green foliage adorning its hilly banks, it looked so clean and fresh and enticing with new scenery to gaze on at every bend, I almost felt like canoeing up the Jutai for a couple of days. By contrast the Amazon was now very uniform khaki in colour, seldom any hills or cliffs, and it had stopped meandering – a point that baffles the experts – a wide expanse of water moving steadily eastwards at an average speed of one and a half knots. The gradient was gentle too, it was less than 300 feet above sea level here.

The next day a large bend in the river offered a maze of alternative routes. The practice on these charts was to put all depths and flow information on what was considered to be the main channel. On other channels, a lot of assumptions seemed to be made, including the course of the channel. The point where the alternative channel left the mainstream and returned to it, was clearly marked but what went on in between was a matter of guess work. As the river split up around a group of islands, only the mainstream appeared to follow a natural course. The alternative channels through the islands were marked very straight, almost like canals. I was caught by this on more than one occasion and often at the expense of a lot of extra work and mileage. Today was such a day and resulted in an hour lost. This in turn meant a fanatical late-afternoon dash to reach my selected camping spot.

In the last minutes of daylight I reached it, threw off my clothes and dived into the river. That one beautiful plunge seemed to make it all worth while: born again was the closest description I could give. A quick wood-gathering operation, some dry clothes on, and a supper of corned beef, water melon and chocolate milk. It was a clear night and I felt optimistic about no storms so I slept without a cover; to watch the stars was a great way to end the day, for there was a clarity here impossible to find over our polluted cities. It made me think of the magnitude of things in space, of stars and galaxies thousands of light years away. This tiny earth is but a speck of dust; I wondered if there were more specks of dust somewhere out there with Amazon-sized rivers on them.

At 0400 on 14th October I was awakened by a light shining on the camp, a passing fisherman with a handlamp. I guessed the kayak was rather conspicuous with its white sides in the moonlight. I flashed my lamp back and he paddled on. I had slept well and I did not mind being woken early.

The island I was on proved interesting and, together with similar islands found later in the trip, gave me a good insight into their age and formation. A chart of this area, drawn up seven years previously, showed nothing more than a sub-surface sandbank here. Sand continued to build up until a low-lying island or sandbank occurred two years later. At this stage, the first grass would appear and within five years there would be an abundance of scrub and a low line of trees. About this time, when the island would have taken on a degree of permanence, it would be given a name. Animals would now be left to graze here periodically and within another five years a family or two would move over. Since crops like bananas take a year or two to be productive, sensible planning would have these ready by the time occupation occurred.

The island I was on was almost certainly of five years' vintage, with scrub and low trees covering much of the surface. Another interesting point was that the island could actually be seen growing vertically. The almost perpetual winds of the area were carrying streams of fine sand and sediment from the new banks forming at the edges of the island up on to the sand dunes of the island itself.

Take off was 0915. A few clouds but generally hot. I thought I had eaten too much porridge this morning and it took almost two hours to get into the swing of things. Everything was OK before midday and progress picked up. By 1400 I was at Fonte Boa, an unusual spot on the river. The town itself was about forty metres above water level, with a concrete stairway leading up. This was the only entrance to the town and it gave the impression of a natural fortress with sheer cliffs for its walls. Most cliffs in the area were a reddish colour and this rather set them apart from typical Amazon scenery.

Fortunately, there were some floating stores at the river's edge and this saved me a lot of climbing. The store owners eyed me sceptically as I read off my shopping list and by the time I had all my supplies loaded, a group of people had become extremely interested in the kayak. Was I really going to Manaus and Belém in that thing? Certainly I was. The store owner's daughter asked if I wanted to eat. Pointing at the food I had, I replied that I would eat later. No, she said, did I want to eat some rice, meat and vegetables? An offer too good to refuse. She was soon back and virtually spoon-fed me whilst I sat in the kayak. Dessert was included, too, much to the annoyance of her boyfriend.

At 1600 I passed a good sandbank but I was feeling lucky and decided to get a few more miles up. By 1745 it was completely dark and no sandbank. However, there was a bank of hardened mud at the eastern peak of Ilha das Araras and that would have to do. The only thing that bothered me was that I could hear cattle. Apart from cows, these islands were often grazed by very large buffalo and to have one of them walk on me in the night was far from desirable. I wedged a few sticks in the ground around the camp, as an early warning system.

A nice breeze picked up so that was the sign for the

mosquitos to go home and I relaxed to a supper of rice pudding and chocolate milk. I had got forty-one nautical miles up today and so I was very happy.

12   INTO TRAFFIC

Towns were more frequent now, but getting into some of them posed problems of navigation and I was nervous of leaving the kayak for too long. On 18th October I reached Alvarães, a medium-sized commercial port with ship repair yards in a beautifully protected bay off a narrow channel, surrounded by tree-covered hills. There were sealed roads and an excellent range of goods, among the best I had found so far. Its only black mark was for the garbage strewn down the river banks. I stocked up with two cans of insect spray, eggs, oats and tinned food, as well as two one-litre plastic water containers which would be strapped to the deck in order not to take up valuable cargo space. I bought them because I felt I might need to carry extra water beyond the Amazon mouth. After reaching Cabo Maguari I planned to proceed down the coast of Ilha Marajo towards Belém.

As usual, the locals had got interested in my kayak and demanded a demonstration. They expressed particular interest in its speed and I had to paddle around the bay for a bit to show them. There were the usual gasps as it nosed through the wake of a passing ship without sinking. At 1400 I was back on the main stream and heading for Tefé.

The sun was blazing and the mirror surface of the river really threw it at me. Just a mouthful of water each hour, remain calm, and pick a speed that does not require too much exertion. With temperatures around 90°F (32°C), it was the only way to handle these conditions. I kept thinking about the crystal-clear water which had cascaded down on me as I had passed through the Pongo Mainiqui. How lovely it would be to find something like that here. At 1530, like an oasis in the desert, I found *Calypso* anchored a few miles out from Tefé: a proven source of cool refreshment.

After a soft drink, followed by a cup of coffee, I had a chat with their newest crew member, a lieutenant-commander from the Brazilian navy who knew the river well. I was especially interested in the tidal areas of the Amazon and the levels of salinity. Although I had read that water was drinkable 200 miles out to sea from the mouth of the Amazon I had rather imagined this was only so in the wet season when flow was at its maximum. The first thing the lieutenant-commander told me was that I could not drink water from the Amazon at all as it was not suitable. I told him I had been drinking nothing else and he looked rather shocked. I hastily added that I boiled it for fifteen minutes or treated it before drinking and this sounded more acceptable to him. "Well, it remains much the same right up to the mouth," he said. So that was good news. I also discussed some of the changes I had noticed in channels and islands. He was well aware of this and mentioned one main channel that had changed its course several times in the past few months. Mme Cousteau handed me three welcome oranges before I set off to find my nightly sandbank.

Without a doubt, I was eating more now. Breakfast was invariably two large plates of porridge, compared to one in the earlier stages of the trip. It was eggs as usual on most days and often fruit. Lunch was sometimes just a couple of biscuits or fruit while I was drifting, and occasionally some tinned food.

I had thought of a new time-saving method for fixing supper. That was to use plenty of water for the rice pudding and add a couple of spoonfuls of chocolate milk powder. When it was all finished, I just drained the excess liquid off into my mug and I had my rice pudding and a chocolate milk drink fixed at the same time. The chocolate flavoured rice pudding was also an improvement.

Tuesday, 20th October dawned superb. As I canoed down the Amazon, I passed from one time zone to another. Today I had to advance my watch one hour to Manaus time. After a standard breakfast, I wrote a letter to the South American Explorers' Club to let them know where I was; hopefully I would find somewhere to post it in the not-too-distant future.

It was 1200 before I took off and an adverse wind kept progress down. I spotted a small village and tried for food and eggs. As I approached the bank, a shotgun went off and two men ducked down behind a bush. I took it as either a scare shot or somebody having a joke. They were about fifty yards distant and could have hit me very easily if they had so desired. The entrance to the village is about a hundred metres on and I pulled up there. I observed people here from a distance, but suddenly there was nobody about. A village of perhaps a hundred people and with armaments decided to vanish when a small kayak pulled on to the beach. I would pay a fair price to know what was going on in the minds of such people. I did not intend following them into the jungle as somebody with a shotgun might get nervous.

To me it was incredible. These people were living on a busy river where large, sometimes very modern ships pass by. Most of them would have been to the larger towns like Tefé or Manaus and some might have actually lived there. They had portable radios in their villages to keep them informed of what was going on in the world. This was not a remote place like those I had passed through at the beginning of my trip. What made a village full of people flee from a plastic kayak?

I made myself a shopping list for Coari, a large town which should have had everything I needed. The shipping was getting busier now as I approached the Amazon mouth, with both cargo and passenger vessels over 1000 tons. There were plenty of floating stores at the water's edge, but I was out of luck, they all dealt in bulk sales to the ships, and the town of Coari proper was too far inland from the river to leave the kayak. However, there was a small village diagonally across the river, so I decided to give it a try instead. My luck returned. I got six eggs. I had not assessed it as more than a two-egg town.

Winds were strong again and the chop remained high. To make matters worse a fairly large passenger boat passing alongside one day suddenly swung back out to midstream, giving me full thrust of its propellers. I do not know if there was any special reason for the manoeuvre but being thrown about by a ship's propellers is not my idea of a joke.

That night I reached a large sandbank, extending half a mile out from the mainland, adjacent to Ilha Jurupari, about thirty miles from Codajas. There was a large horizontal tree-trunk here so I used it to make a full camp. I got some clothes washed and the camp fire blazing. I also used the large log as my table, conveniently spreading food containers upon it.

One disadvantage of having large camp fires is the inability to see into the darker areas around you. Now I almost walked into someone hanging round the camp. How long he had been watching me I do not know but he was standing by the log where I had spread out all my gear. He showed me a turtle he had in a bag and said he was out hunting for them along the bank. That was probably true, but was no reason for him to hang about my camp. He wandered off and I continued with my cooking.

The mosquitos were dense for the first hour of darkness but tapered off soon after. Perhaps this was due to a combination of things, including having a nice cool wash before supper, putting some dry clothes on and spraying the camp area and myself with repellent. I had still not devised a foolproof solution for the mosquito problem, but these things helped.

I was 221 nautical miles up this week, eleven above average. My actual mileage was probably closer to 300, but chasing food supplies or doing extra miles around unmarked sand-banks was not taken into consideration. The only mileage I counted was downstream towards my destination.

To keep up my weekly average was costing me more and more work under increasingly adverse conditions. The only effect this was having on me at the moment was to make me eat more to produce the extra calories. The amount of porridge I got through every day was steadily increasing.

By 2100 I was into bed and soon fast asleep. A flashlamp shining on the camp in the early hours of the morning woke me. I climbed out of the sleeping-sack and found the turtle hunter shining his lamp over the kayak. When he saw me get out from under the cover, he started to repeat the names scrawled on the side of the kayak. He had seen them earlier but was trying to justify his being there. When he saw that I was not impressed, he opened the bag to show me the turtle again, pointing in the direction he had caught it. I looked at my watch and told him the hour. He then strolled off.

Later in the day I found a tin of insect spray missing – the only loss from the camp since the start of the trip and one of the few things I now left out at night just in case the mosquitos got too thick. Even wet clothes were put in plastic bags and packed in the kayak till dawn. I could not afford to lose essential equipment.

Sunday, 24th October brought clear skies and without a

doubt a hot day to follow. There had been another dramatic change in the river here. The main channel should be close to the northern bank but had moved a mile or so across and was now following the southern bank. The main channel would usually give you around 100 feet of depth, considerably more in places, so even the largest passenger boats could get through. The only problem for them was knowing where that channel was at any given time. There is no absolute right of way on the river. It is just an unwritten law that vessels proceeding upstream take the area of least current, typically the inside of bends, and downstream vessels follow the maximum flow. This means that vessels will be zig-zagging from side to side of the river, depending on whether the river bends to the left or right. Apart from the large port areas, there were no markers or buoys. Occasionally, the chart would mark a conspicuous tree or peak from which to take a bearing but not much else.

By late afternoon and close to dark, I reached Codajas, a large commercial town. Being Sunday, almost everything was closed, including all the waterside stores. I pulled the kayak ashore near the passenger-boat terminal and climbed the bank to town. It was hell to pull up in these places in a kayak, as there were broken bottles and rusty tins everywhere. Apart from the scraping and graunching poor ol' kayak got, the dangers of serious foot injury were high.

A quick stroll up main street and I spotted a snack bar open. The owner did not sell much that I needed but he was a great source of information on where I could find it. For good measure, he sent his young shop assistant along to help me. The store had the works: tinned food, eggs, oats, sugar, rice, milk powder. I offered the shop assistant a small tip for showing me the place but he declined the offer.

So back I went down the bank, struggling to keep hold of all the supplies at the same time. A passenger boat had just pulled in and a large crowd had gathered around my kayak. They watched in fascination as I crammed all the supplies into every conceivable space. My plastic egg box proved to be a great source of amusement. As I was pulling away, one man asked, "Are you well armed?" I just smiled and paddled on. No one followed.

It was almost glassy calm and I put the pressure on to distance myself from the town and find somewhere for the night. Within twenty minutes the last light faded and things did not look too good. There was a half moon which would have been a reasonable source of light had it not been for the misty conditions on the river. As the large boats passed, I nosed the kayak towards their wake. Getting it side on in the dark would not be fun. Steep banks everywhere with no promise of a beach. At 2000 the mist increased and I was getting concerned. It now became difficult to spot the waves from passing ships and I was sometimes caught unaware; the odd boil-up would almost have me over as I was trying to eye the bank. Ships' searchlights were sometimes helpful, sometimes not. They used extremely powerful lamps to scan the river and banks, which gave me clues to likely camp spots. Then they would spot me and hold the lamp on me for five to ten seconds, trying to work out whether I was a bit of driftwood or not. It takes about thirty minutes to get effective night vision and just a few seconds with a searchlight to lose it again.

By 2030 conditions further deteriorated and a large vessel was coming too near for comfort. I moved as close as I could into the bank to keep clear of its propellers. I feared getting hit with both the oncoming and reflected waves at the same time, but I did not see that I had much choice. God must have smiled for me because I found a small cove as the ship passed. It was quite small, barely 100 feet across but its narrow harbour-like entrance saved me. I slipped in as the waves pounded the banks. After that I knew I must be in God's good books for the day. Not only was it a safe cove, but it had a nice sandbank beneath its far wall.

Corned beef, chocolate rice pudding and chocolate milk for supper and with thirty-eight miles up, it was the end of a satisfying day. I had to do some more rebalancing of the cargo, also a few repairs and a full check of water seepage and cargo condition. So I decided tomorrow would be allocated to those tasks.

By daylight I discovered the cove was ideal. There was a reasonable amount of dead wood dropped from the overhanging trees which should afford me some shade to work under. Another little bonus was a tiny trickle of clear water seeping from the rear wall of the cove. Crystal-clear water is magical stuff to look at after spending so much time looking at the khaki-coloured Amazon. It took around half an hour to fill a one-litre container but there was no rush.

These little coves are another feature of the changing Amazon. The constant pounding of the soft banks by the river wears them away. There are very few hard stones or rocks to contend with, so erosion of the banks is fairly rapid. It is also enhanced by the river traffic, invariably busy near the larger towns. But somewhere downstream, another bank or island will be forming to take its place. The most incredible part of it all is the sheer volume of sediment that gets dragged down towards the sea each day: three million cubic metres of aluvium. It was almost as if a continent was moving before my eyes.

At 0800 a spear-fisherman drifted downstream and into the cove. These were the spots the fish hung out and he knew how to find them. His young son kept the dugout steady whilst he stood at the bow watching for the tell-tale movements. He was remarkably skilled. A spear through the head of a fish it was not possible to see. I climbed to the top of the ledge overlooking the fishing spot to see if I could analyse how it was done. A few small fish would leap from the water in an arc of 180 degrees. This told him the direction of the attack. Then a swirl of disturbance as the larger fish made a thrust towards its selected victims. Absolutely nothing of the big fish was visible. It was just the ability of the fisherman to read water and strike at the right moment. It was a monster he caught, a type of large cod, weighing around fifty kilos. After taking photos, I gave the young son some fishing hooks and the father my spring-balance. I knew the weights of virtually all my cargo now and I had no further use for it. He asked me what I wanted for it, so I told him to bring me a melon next time he passed. He agreed and said he would be back tomorrow morning.

I recoated the spray cover with silicone rubber and left it to set. Next I repaired the front carry-handle. Its rope had almost frayed away. The cockpit combing had worked itself loose in parts and some maintenance had to be done here also. The bracket for my wave-deflector had been damaged a bit and I doubted its usefulness: it might get torn free on impact with a large roller. The kayak had handled reasonably well without it so far and I decided to carry on without it. I'd tried it out on a few occasions and found the constant spray thrown back into my face every time it impacted a wave to be annoying.

I laid most of the cargo out and apart from minor dampness it seemed to be in good order. The hatches had remained watertight. Some money I kept in my wallet was beginning to rot again and so that had to be laid out in the sun and dried once more.

By midday the sweat was pouring off me and I had to climb further up the bank to get shade from the trees. By early afternoon shadows crept across the camp and I carried on with the work. There was a fair amount of algae growth on the lower parts of the kayak, probably slowing me up a bit. However, I decided to leave removing that for the water's edge where I could use sand and soap as an abrasive. Otherwise, apart from a couple of areas on the bottom which were wearing a little thin, the kayak seemed to be in fair condition.

I reloaded the cargo and made a couple of shopping lists of long-term and short-term items. The two kilos of oats on board would last me fourteen days at present consumption rates. However, I intended re-stocking with this as opportunities presented themselves. I still had almost 200 saccharine tablets for sweetening but preferred to keep them for emergency while sugar was available; they were very compact and took up virtually no room. Half of my freeze-dried food remained in storage for eating as I approached Cabo Maguari. They were still the most ideal emergency supplies I had and would be used sparingly. My solar panel was no longer charging the batteries properly but it had served its purpose. I could now buy disposable ones.

Strong winds woke me on 26th October and a storm drill was necessary. The winds kept up for thirty minutes followed by a small shower before it all tapered away. I got the fire going for breakfast and a different spear-fisherman from yesterday pulled into the cove with two melons. He carried them to the top of the bank and like some amateur salesman started to tell me how delicious they were "How much do you want for them?" I asked. A thousand cruzeiros for two, was the answer. So I told him what to do with the melons and he left.

Perhaps word had got round that I had given a good spring-balance away for nothing and had no sense of values. A thousand cruzeiros for two melons was five times the going price. About an hour later my friend from yesterday returned and gave me a melon for nothing.

Manacapuru was much the same as Codajas but gave the appearance of being more grotty. Broken glass and bottles right down to the water's edge and a slum at the east end of town. The rubbish tip was the river bank as usual, gradually rotting and sliding into the river. Great caution had to be taken in collecting water near these towns. I either collected it well before reaching them or as far downstream from them as possible. The amount of pollution caused by these rubbish tips on a river of such magnitude as the Amazon was of course insignificant. But a noticeably murky appearance and some foul odours were always apparent at the waterfronts though the local people thought nothing of taking their water direct from the river here.

I was able to get everything I needed at the waterfront stores, batteries, eggs, oats, and was on my way again by 1330. A slight increase in winds and a small storm that I did not have to stop for and by 1830 I reached a large sandbank at the western peak of Ilha Maria Antonio.

I was now about twenty nautical miles from the junction of the Amazon and Negro rivers. There was some tricky water there and I wanted to be sure I would pass it in daylight. The Negro is a large black-water river around 1000 miles long and its meeting with the Amazon is spectacular for the two rivers ride side by side for many miles without mixing. However, great forces are at work beneath the surface as the rivers collide and large whirlpools are frequent.

I was too tired to gather wood and light a fire, so it was corned beef and biscuits for supper. At 2030 I lay down to sleep. To hell with building a camp. Skies were clear and I had decided it was not going to rain.

13 DAMN THOSE WINDS

On 29th October I was awake at 0530. This was the day I was to negotiate the junction of the river Negro, a massive tributary of the Amazon, with the busy city of Manaus at the confluence. The term 'black water' in the Amazon region is generally given to any river that contrasts with the tawny colour of the Amazon, though these rivers are often relatively clear or translucent. The Amazon incidentally is referred to as a white-water river. The Negro is black because of all the humic acids dissolved in its water. These in turn inhibit the reproduction of insect life, including the nasty little mosquito. Manaus, being on the Negro, has mosquito-free beaches which are very popular. How much nicer my trip would have been if God had made all the Amazon black too!

I needed to get across to the south bank of the river, but the strong easterly wind was upsetting the flow, causing large rollers and white caps. I had to make a gradual ferry-glide type crossing, taking two and a half hours to do it, and arriving ten miles downstream. It was good experience, as I could expect much more of these conditions beyond Manaus. I had a slice of water melon and pressed on to the Negro-Amazon junction. There was some tricky water about, but visibility was good and I kept a constant scan in all directions for trouble.

I could see old Manaus across the river, but had no desire to stop as I had been there three years before. Manaus was originally established as a garrison post and mission in the seventeenth century. With a population approaching half a million, it is the capital of the state of Amazonas. Sumptuous buildings and an opera house built on European lines are witness to its prosperous times at the turn of the century during the great rubber boom. The monopoly was finally broken by the development of the Malaysian plantations. Now a tax-free port served by ocean-going vessels and boasting a supersonic airport, it has become the nation's smuggling capital.

I now had about 1000 miles left to cover which should take me a month. Tides would be a new problem to contend with on this leg of the trip and I might have to synchronise my travelling time with them to maintain effective daily mileage. They could be 'sensed' as far up as Manaus but their real force would be felt beyond Santarém. I was reasonably happy with things up to Macapá but beyond that I would have to contend with the direct influence of the Atlantic, in particular with the Pororoca, a mystery about which I had been unable to get any satisfying answers.

The name 'Pororoca', given to it by the Indians, means 'big roar'. It is an area at the mouth of the Amazon where the river meets the ocean and causes twelve-foot-high tidal bores. A breaking wall of water races upstream with a deafening roar and menaces all shipping in its path. The most authoritative books say little more than that it occurs when certain conditions are favourable and is caused by forces not fully understood. How to predict the Pororoca and what to do about it was even more of a mystery.

Next morning winds were slight so I got under way. The great god of thunder must have been pleased to see me do that and blackened the sky. I kept going but scanned the banks for emergency pull-ins. Soon the sandstorms from far-off banks gave their warning and I made for a cove. Dangerous winds were on me within minutes and the waves were pounding against the banks. The cove was not the best in the circumstances as its opening faced on to the full force of the storm. I dragged the kayak up on to a mudbank, sinking knee-deep in ooze as I did this.

There was a settlement here and it was not long before people came to see what I was up to. I pointed to the storm and told them I would be off in fifteen minutes. The rains never came but the full force of the wind did, slamming great rollers up the bank and swamping the cockpit with muddy water. As usual, in fifteen minutes it was over, and now it was just a wait until the turbulence settled. But I was getting too much unwanted advice from mouthy youths on the bank above who did not know one end of a kayak from another, so I got tired of their suggestions and made off.

The main channel followed this bank and the winds had

upset it considerably. I have never seen a river that could get so violently upset by just fifteen minutes of strong winds. Whether it is the sheer magnitude of flow the wind is trying to oppose, I do not know, but the Amazon reacts violently to easterlies. I have seen small passenger boats swing into banks and put people off for fear of being swamped. The Amazon just did not like being disturbed. So I had fifteen minutes of nasty water to contend with, including a couple of whirls, until the water gradually ironed out again.

Progress was good but spotting sandbanks was hampered by a continuous vertical bank, either adorned with trees or cleared for settlement, which rose above my head.

By 1730 the nearest likely spot I could see was about five miles diagonally across the river from me and with only half an hour's daylight left, that would mean getting my finger out. A quick check showed clear skies, river now almost glassy calm, close to a full moon tonight; everything said yes, so off I went. The last rays of the sun kept the bank illuminated for about half the distance and by then I had sorted out a couple of markers beyond the bank to guide me in. As the bank faded, I found myself going faster and faster to try and keep it in focus. It is a battle I seldom win: light fades too fast. I then used my marker trees to guide me in and watch for drift. It was a lovely bank to find on a Saturday night, soft, dry, virgin sand and not a soul in sight. After dragging ol' kayak ashore, another pleasant surprise. No mosquitos! I can only believe this is due to the proximity and influence of the river Negro.

This, incidentally, made me think back to other isolated mosquito-free nights on the trip. Was another black-water river or creek nearby at the time? It was possible.

I stripped off and enjoyed a bath in the river and then strolled around in the moonlight gathering wood until I was dry. The bank was about half a mile diameter, and fairly new, only low scrub existed here and very little that was suitable for fire wood. However, that was the least of my worries. Finding a bank like this was paradise in itself.

For supper it was sausages, rice pudding and chocolate milk. It was such a lovely evening that I stayed up later than usual to enjoy it. I had covered 217 nautical miles this week and that is seven above target. Not bad considering I only canoed six days. At 2230 I turned in. Just an open camp – no cover.

On 31st October I awoke at dawn, 0530, and spent half an hour doing nothing, just enjoying the peace and tranquillity. At 0600 I crawled out of the sack and inhaled a few breaths of the Amazon's perfumed fragrance. There was a light breeze blowing and a few flimsy clouds. After hanging the washing out, I gathered wood for breakfast. The birds thought I was after their eggs and kicked up their usual fuss. What makes them choose open banks to lay eggs on I will never know. Wood was really scarce and I had to make do with piles of scrub grass.

I'd had a slight dysentery problem for two days now and I could not figure out why. The answer came when I opened another tin of sausages. A loud hissing noise. They were blown. I remembered a similar noise from the tin I ate near Manaus. I should have heeded the warning.

After breakfast, I was checking my charts when a couple of farmers came across to the bank from an adjacent island. They brought a cow with them and a bundle of fencing stakes. They walked past my camp but never spoke. I honestly think I had worried them into believing that I was settling here.

I am not sure of the system of laying claim to these banks or islands, but from this incident and other similar ones, I think it is just a question of justifying your presence by planting crops or putting animals on it to graze. There was nothing on this island when I arrived, nor was it likely that anything had been here before, as it was still in a very early stage of development. A couple of cows would probably eat it out in as many days. Not to worry – he could ship his cow back when I was gone.

At 1100 I was on my way and it was intermittent winds and rain to contend with from there on. Lots of short stops but little by little I got the miles up. By nightfall I had not spotted anything suitable for camp and a storm was brewing. Skies were black, the moon was covered and winds were increasing. There was a beach near to a small settlement on the north bank of the river, so I pulled over to sit the storm out.

A church service was just finishing and I had been spotted coming in. A powerful flashlamp was shone down at me and I just waved back. I sat in the kayak eating biscuits, but the man with the flashlamp was terribly concerned. He came within thirty feet, still holding the lamp on me. I told him I was waiting for the storm to pass before continuing on towards Santarém. He started to come a little closer when a woman higher up the bank called out to him to stop and come away. He panicked and ran up the bank. It made me wonder what they had learned at church today. Perhaps Satan was touring the Amazon in a kayak, eating biscuits? Ten minutes later, a posse had gathered. With a couple more flashlights, a few stiff drinks in their hands, down they came. Still sitting in my kayak, I showed them my charts and where I was heading. After a few questions they seemed happier and since winds had tapered off now, I decided to move on.

The next day, 1st November, started sunny but soon became overcast. I was unable to dry any clothes or air my sleeping-sack. By 1200 I was at Itacoatiara. No less than a hundred ships tied up here, most of them small, fifty to a hundred tons, and many in for repairs. There was a busy timber mill nearby, supplying wood for ship repairs but not much commercial activity on the waterfront. At the downstream end of town, melons were being loaded on to a horse and cart and that was my only purchase for the day.

I travelled on for another twenty miles and again had problems finding a bank. Zig-zagging across the river was a thankless task – it was about three miles wide here. I would often get to the far side of the river, only to find that what had looked a promising bank at a distance was in fact anything but. I finally had to settle on a muddy patch at the tail end of the island. It was quite useless to wash, as I had to wade knee-deep in mud to get to the water. It was hard ground where the camp was but generally uncomfortable surroundings.

Some fishermen in a motor launch and four dugouts work-ing as a team appeared very interested in me. The dugouts were drifting with the current and fishing whilst the motor launch periodically gathered them up and took them back upstream. By dusk, they had had enough and anchored alongside my camp. I introduced myself and told them of my expedition. They looked at my kayak and equipment with evident suspi-cion. I was not concerned and got the fire going for supper. They cooked their supper on the motor launch and continued to talk about me, frequently referring to me as a 'bandido'. I told them again that I came from Australia and was on an expedition. The next murmurs I heard were 'Australian *bandido*'! Why was it so easy for a Peruvian to work out I was on an expedition and yet so difficult for a Brazilian? Peruvians had quickly realised that the kayak and equipment were not manufactured in Peru and obviously had to be imported at considerable expense. Common sense then prevailed. Anyone spending that kind of money did not come all this way to rob a few villages of their pots, pans and bananas! There were unlikely to be enough items of enough value to pay for the paddle, never mind the kayak! In Peru, that would usually be the end of the assessment and it was then *bon voyage*, a friendly wave, and we would part company. Why so few people in Brazil were able to pursue that line of logic, I do not know.

On 3rd November I crossed the river again to stock up at the town of Urucurituba. I was surprised at the turbulence as I made a diagonal crossing. The river narrowed at this point and everything got thrust out to midstream for a bumpy ride, with logs and debris everywhere.

Despite having almost a dozen shops the range of goods was poor, and Urucurituba proved to be only a three-egg town. There was a bit of ship repair going on, mainly replacement of timbers from old wooden cargo boats. I watched them work for a while and the impression I got was that the skills were more of the hand-me-down type than those taught at school, the trained eye being more important than precision measurements. A large crowd came down to see me off. All were friendly and it helped make the day.

Winds were still moderate and progress was fair. By early afternoon I had got my extra three eggs from a small village I passed. Winds were abating and by mid-afternoon, it was almost glassy calm. Hunger pangs were gnawing at me again, so I decided to have a tin of corned beef. The extra effort needed each day was certainly showing on my food bills.

I was really enjoying this little snack whilst drifting downstream, in fact I was enjoying it so much I even took my feet out of the cockpit and put them up on the foredeck. The kayak tends to drift stern first, owing to the extra drag caused by the fin. It was therefore occasionally necessary to peer over my shoulder to see that I was not heading into any logs or obstructions. I browsed over the map and worked out my estimated camp spot for the night and carried on eating. What I had not noticed was the narrowing of the channel I was in as I passed between the south bank and an adjacent island. The island broadened towards its downstream end, causing a further restriction and a considerable increase in flow. Without warning, the kayak started to spin, the first two turns slowly but then picked up rapidly. I slammed the corned beef down and dug the paddle in for all I was worth. "Move, you bloody idiot, move." A large whirlpool was forming and I was close to the eye of it. I paddled for all I was worth away from the centre and clear of its grasp. Once fully formed, it would not have had the slightest problem swallowing both the kayak and me. I watched it pass on downstream, sucking in all logs and debris in its path. The Amazon never allows you to relax for long.

By 1730 I had got thirty-three nautical miles up and found a low bank at a bend on the river. Very little wood but one large trunk to make camp against. The bark had started to fall away from it, so I levered large sections off for the fire. The loose bark worried me a little as there were wide enough gaps behind it for snakes to live. But soon there was a dull thud as a king-sized frog hopped out and landed on the bank. He was the largest one I have ever seen and would weigh at least a kilo. Using my paddle, I shunted him along to a nearby pool, clear of the camp.

The mosquitos were around by nightfall but lacking their usual intensity. A bigger nuisance tonight was the bats. They were swooping and fluttering around my face and head for the whole night. Their radar system was remarkably good. I tried swiping a few of them with a paddle but they managed to avoid it. Judging by the amount of interest they were showing, I would suspect they were vampire bats, not quite as dangerous as their B-movie reputation but, given the opportunity, they will suck blood from a human, and some carry rabies.

It was corned beef, rice pudding and chocolate milk for supper and bed by 2130.

At 0500 next morning, there was a sudden thump on the sleeping-sack that felt as if a cat had jumped on it. I did not bother investigating – I knew what it would be. I gave a kick to the area where it had landed and it hopped off again. It was just the frog returning home.

At 0530 I got up and fixed breakfast. Some dolphins were splashing around near the bank and I took some movie film. To the best of my knowledge, nobody hunts the dolphin in the Amazon but they remain very cautious of boats and people, more so than their salt-water cousins. I had often had them swim around the kayak, but seldom at less than thirty feet distance.

I was off at 1115 and winds were light to moderate as I crossed to the northern bank of the river. There was some lovely scenery here: red and white cliffs, their tops adorned with lush green vegetation. Occasionally a small hut or dwelling concealed in a cove at the base. The privilege of living in such surroundings would more than compensate for being outside the money economy. Coconut palms waved in the breeze, it was most picturesque. A 1000-ton cargo vessel passed close by, with a blast on the horn and a friendly wave from the crew.

Late in the afternoon of 5th November I'd reached a position opposite Parintins but was having problems locating a camp site. Darkness was falling and I did not really want to cross the river in these conditions. However, the only likely camp spots appeared to be on the south bank. A few more minutes checking the north bank out and I decided I would have to cross – I had to sleep somewhere.

Using the lights of town to correct for drift, I made my way over. The flow was strong in the centre and had me sweating to keep on course. Things improved towards the south bank. I used the eddies to get back upstream to the camp spot, about two miles further on. As luck would have it, it was just a hard brown clay bank and not the soft sand I had imagined it to be. Win a few, lose a few; it would have to do.

I pulled the kayak up and almost stepped on a black snake. Using my paddle, I ejected it well out into the river. It looked much better out there! I scanned the whole area with the flashlamp just in case I was in some kind of snakes' home! There was no other activity, so I set up camp. It was a bit near the town and rather than invite attention, I had a cold supper of corned beef and melon. The ground was rock hard and I did not expect a very comfortable night but I had learned to be grateful for small mercies. It was a place to sleep.

The river became active at an early hour, with motor boats and even sailing boats coming upstream. The sailboats were basically large dugouts or planked row-boats with a stout bamboo pole for a mast and something resembling a bed sheet for a sail. Others were using nothing more than a polythene sheet as a type of spinnaker to pull them upstream to work. Most were not going far, just to work the farms along the bank.

At Parintins a large number of Amazon passenger boats were tied up. They are strange-looking craft, like a double-decker bus with a barge for a wheel base, and a very shallow draught which allows them to come close into the shore. They look like descendants of the old Mississippi paddle steamers and it's not difficult to imagine a paddle wheel on to the stern. A large vessel might take a hundred passengers and run between Manaus and Belém in four days. Sleeping accommodation is usually in hammocks strung in rows across the deck. In rough weather this can be both a rocky and an intimate experience.

By early evening I made camp on the mainland. No sandy beaches around so I had to drag the kayak over a mudbank to a dry patch beyond. I had made 210 miles for the week and that was exactly on target. However, with increasing winds against me, I now wondered how much longer I could keep that up.

At night I watched the huge tankers and cargo vessels labouring upstream. They look rather beautiful, well lit up, their powerful searchlights scanning the river methodically, a few seconds starboard, a few straight ahead and then a few to port. There was nothing haphazard about the way these large vessels were handled. They set the impression of having very disciplined and responsible crews.

Sunday, 7th November was dry but cloudy and soon the easterlies would pick up. Judging by the number of sailing boats I had seen between Parintins and here, I could now take the winds for granted. Even moderate-sized motorised cargo boats were using sails for extra fuel economy on the upstream leg.

14 DUCKING BULLETS

I am turning into an Austrian bandit! Young kids along the
bank, seeing probably their first-ever kayak, murmur, '*Bandido!*' And when I stop to buy supplies I find these people have
some difficulty in understanding Australia. Most confuse it
with Austria and assume I speak *Alemao* (German). I often
draw little maps in the sand and try to explain the difference
between Austria and Australia, but I seldom get the message
through.

By midday on 8th November I was passing Ilha Bicheira, just
five nautical miles north-east of Juruti. The area south of the
island opened out in to a wide sandy bay about half a mile
across. There was no protection from the wind here. I was
driving directly into it. So I moved out from the shore to cut
diagonally across the bay. I noticed a young man running
along the beach in the direction of some boats with what
appeared to be a paddle in his hand. He was about fifty yards
from me when he passed the boats and I took a second look at
what he was carrying. It was not a paddle but a shotgun or rifle
and he seemed in a desperate hurry to get somewhere and use
it. I scanned further up the bank to see if I could spot what he
was after. There were two large birds about another 150 yards
on, so perhaps he was after them. He was running through
creeks and streams like a man possessed, chest-high in water,
holding the gun above his head. As time passed I grew more
suspicious of him and adjusted my course. After he had run
past where the birds were, I had no more doubts about his
intentions. He was trying to get as far round the bay as possible
so I would be downwind from him. I immediately made out for
midstream and when he saw that there was no more advantage
in following the bay round, he raised the gun and opened fire. I
made as narrow a profile as possible by turning the kayak end
on to him, and crouched forward wrapping my arms around
my face.

I was about 150 yards from him at this time and this

164

distance, combined with the cross wind, made the shot ineffective. It would be hard to express my anger at that moment.
Anybody who can judge and pass sentence on a person he had
never spoken to nor seen commit any crime is an irrational
maniac who shouldn't be allowed to possess a gun. I watched
him break it and remove the spent shell, his sorry profile
expressing his regret at having missed. In anger I yelled, "Son
of a bitch" at him and he yelled something in return. The winds
were too strong to make either statement intelligible. Without
a gun, that imbecile could have done nothing more than jump
up and down on the beach.

I stayed well clear of the banks now and pushed on downstream. By 1715 I had forty miles up and made camp.

During supper I thought over the days' events and what a
fine thread my life was hanging on. Even if I had only been
wounded in the incident, my chances of survival would have
been very slim. It required considerable effort just to keep a
kayak stable under these windy conditions and if I had ended
up in the Amazon streaming blood, the death would have been
far from pleasant. This incident has taken something from the
trip.

Next day as I made for Óbidos an open motor boat with no
less than ten grown men in it pulled out from a settlement and
followed me downstream. And there, standing at the bow in
full John Wayne stance was the great Mario, shotgun slanting
down at me, two rows of cartridge belts slung across his
shoulders. What a hero! What a great show, and all for a
plastic kayak that was probably carrying 1000 kilos of contra-
band bananas! I could not help thinking they should have sent
Mario to the Falklands. He could have settled the dispute
single-handed!

The boat pulled alongside and asked where I was heading. I
pointed to the clearly visible directions marked on the sides.
"Don't you see, I'm on an expedition. I am heading for
Belém." My arrogance seemed to embarrass them into silence:
there was now an embarrassed realisation that things had been
overdone.

I paddled on, still uncertain whether I would cop a blast
from the shotgun. I was really disgusted. I was in full agree-
ment with people policing their village but why can common

sense not prevail? Ten men and enough armaments to go to war, for somebody in a little plastic kayak with a plastic paddle in his hands. I had met official police on the river and in the towns: I was yet to have one pull a gun on me. These local militia tended to get carried away with the limited authority granted to them.

By 1200 I was opposite Óbidos and stopped for a snack. It was quite a pleasant sight, a bluff overlooking the river, it was easy to see why the Portuguese had built a fort there.

I did not need any stores so I carried on down the south side of the river which was well populated with lots of small villages; finding a camp spot would not be easy. I was amused by a small cargo boat which stopped at each settlement to sell melons; it must have been a daily run as queues of women were waiting at each halt, purses in hand. I purchased a melon and asked about banks in the area.

By 1730 I had not found anything so I decided to go in and talk to the locals. Two horsemen came down to the bank to see what I wanted; both had rifles secured forward of the saddle. I told them about my expedition and asked if it would be OK if I stopped there for the night. They said there was no problem but it would not be very comfortable. A few of the villagers came down to see me and the horsemen told them of my intention. They seemed agreeable and I gave one of them the remainder of the fishing line I had, about seventy metres. I also showed my documents to the two horsemen and they discreetly cautioned me not to hand them over to the villagers. These two fellows were much better dressed than the villagers and either owned the land here or had considerable influence in the area. They were nice enough and before leaving, offered me some fish for supper. This I politely declined.

So I set up camp on the hard clay beach, much to the amusement of the dozen or so locals who stood by and watched. It was just a basic camp with groundsheet and sleeping-sack. A youth brought me a free water melon which was consumed along with the rice pudding for supper.

At 2200 two local drunks came to the camp wanting money for spirits. One was the man I had given the fishing line to and he stank of something resembling petrol. They tripped over everything and kept showing me the empty bottle. I could be pretty sure that that was where the fishing line had gone.

Next morning I was on my way by 0520. Winds had been blowing hard all night but had now abated so I wanted to make maximum use of the lull. At 0800 a small cargo boat pulled alongside and handed me a free water melon, wishing me *bon voyage*. By what standard could I judge these people? Kind, generous, logical, irrational, homicidal, compassionate? I was yet to find common ground. Perhaps the multiracial mixing pot hasn't been going long enough to produce a homogeneous Brazilian.

On 11th November I made a long angular crossing towards the south bank and the major town of Santarém. The bottom of the kayak slapped on every wave so regularly that it gave me a headache. I reached the junction of the Tapajos and Amazon rivers just after midday and headed into town.

The Tapajos, sometimes referred to as a green or clear-water river, was a pleasant contrast to the Amazon. As I crossed the dividing line of the two rivers I experienced a sudden perception of depth. It did not matter how far I put my paddle down, I could still see it crystal clear, quite a shock after spending months on murky water into which I could not see more than a few inches. I can remember thinking aloud, "Christ, it's deep here" – a strange thought considering most of the Brazilian section of the Amazon exceeds 120 feet.

The name of the river is taken from the original inhabitants of the area, the Tapajos Indians. Apart from being skilled in making pottery, they also built roads some of which are still in existence today.

Santarém had changed since my last visit. New piers were being constructed and a lot of fresh development was going on in the town. Having lower water levels also effected a change for the better. A broad sandy beach brightened up the town frontage. I pulled the kayak up to this and chased around the stores for a few more supplies. I did not need much, just eggs, biscuits and milk powder. Oranges were being sold along the beach, an unexpected bonus, so I bought twenty and stuffed them into the hatches.

By 1400 it was time to go again and as soon as I had got my spray cover secure, all the young kids on the beach decided to assist me with a fast take-off. Grinning and laughing, they pushed for all they were worth, secretly hoping I would capsize.

Next day conditions were bad and I had to make frequent stops to mop and pump the cockpit out. At the same time, I had to battle to keep the nose into the rollers and stop the kayak from broaching to. About midday I almost ran into a crocodile splashing around in the surf. He was not so big and I had a better understanding of them now. I did not change course for him, I just told him to get out the !*** way and that's exactly what he did.

As I reached the downstream end of the Ilha Nova, a motor boat with six men in it pulled alongside, asking for documents. Since none was wearing a uniform, I asked to see their documents before they had any right to check mine. They could not produce a piece of toilet paper between them but kept insisting that I had to go back to their village to have my cargo checked. I argued with them for a while longer but it proved futile as one man tied a rope to the front carry-handle and tried to pull me along. I cut this with my knife but the others managed to grab the kayak. The situation was hopeless; I would have to go along with them.

Fifteen minutes later we were at their village, Campanha, and I told them to go and get an authorised police representative. They could not find anyone. "He's gone fishing," they told me. "You will have to wait till he returns." Since there was no police representative in the village, I would have liked to have known who endowed them with powers of arrest.

It was 1700 and getting close to dark before an old man of about sixty, Señor Waldomiro Coelho, arrived. He seemed a decent bloke and I handed him the Brazilian consul's letter and my passport. His eyesight was fading so he handed the letter to a younger man who was semi-illiterate and stumbled through it word by word. Then the old man wanted to see the cargo, so I started to unpack the kayak. As he inspected each item and was satisfied with it, he placed it in the cockpit. The other men would then pick it up and pass it around. If it was something like a camera, you could be sure they would adjust and turn every knob and setting. What that had to do with checking cargo, I do not know. In order to keep track of my possessions, I had repeatedly to stop them picking things up and keep reminding them that only one of them was a police representative.

After thirty minutes Señor Coelho was satisfied and I repacked the gear. A knife and some camera batteries were missing but all denied knowledge of them. I got the police officer to sign a statement giving the time and place of my being there, purely for record purposes. Two young men were continually cadging for money. I told them that I thought they were nothing more than a pair of bandits. They disgusted me.

It was dark when I left and I still had to find a camp spot. I proceeded downstream for a couple of miles and then pulled on to a beach. I was too angry to make a camp. I just needed a few hours' rest before getting clear of the place. I munched oranges and biscuits for supper and lay on the groundsheet beside the kayak. I had made my mind up now; foul weather or not, I was staying out in midstream for the rest of the trip, coming in only to sleep or buy provisions at the larger towns.

The river was about three miles wide here and next morning I made straight for midstream. Winds and chop varied throughout the day but progress was fair, and just before dusk I pulled in to a small beach, at the extreme eastern end of the Ilhas do Cucari, a large group of islands through which I have been travelling much of the day.

With my fire burning in a small pit to conceal its light I organised the camp and started to prepare supper. Suddenly I heard branches snapping and a great thumping and crashing amongst the trees: it sounded like an elephant gone wild. Suddenly it came out and froze in its tracks just a few feet from me. It was the largest buffalo I had ever seen in my life. It was a monster and it just stood there, snorting and glaring at me. There was nowhere I could go; even if the kayak had been packed, it would have been a useless gesture to try to run. I grabbed hold of the largest stick I could find and smashed it against a log, yelling at the top of my voice. The buffalo took off and I sighed with relief.

I met more buffaloes on other islands. They are not indigenous animals, being originally imported by the Portuguese and now a cross between European and Indian stock. Some are domesticated, but others roam wild and can be vicious when surprised. I selected my island camp sites with great caution from now on.

It was difficult to say what effects the tides were having in this area. There was about a three-foot-level change but it was possibly not much more than a build-up of water rather than a reverse flow. With the rough conditions it was impossible to detect flow direction. If I stopped paddling, I got pushed back upstream at around two knots, regardless of which way the tide was going.

Over the next two days the swell increased. By itself, the large swell was no problem. It was when the rollers turned into breakers and tried to turn you over, end on end, that the dangerous part came. I might get four rollers in a row and suddenly the fifth one would steepen and break as I was coming up its side. The cockpit had to be pumped out every two hours and the well-worn spray cover was letting in more and more water each day.

As the wind increased I kept an eye over my shoulder for shipping as I was not likely to hear them coming. I was slogging it out in midstream when I spotted three large warships coming down. They were going full bore with their bows a mass of foam. They were almost directly behind me and there was not much I could do to change course. I had to keep facing downstream into the rollers or get rolled. The only way to reach either bank was the slow process of ferry-gliding across but there was no time for that. It was unlikely they would spot me amidst the white caps. That was the whole idea of my being out here in the first place.

When they were within 500 yards they appeared to be slightly to my left so I started to ferry-glide right. The thrust on those damn things must have been phenomenal, foam spewing across the foredeck as they forced their way through the rollers. All three were in line and the first passed me on the port side within 150 feet. They were patrol vessels of the Brazilian navy. Somebody on the bridge spotted me as they passed, possibly their first sighting. I doubt that even a radar would pick up a fibreglass kayak amidst such hectic water conditions.

Now large rollers from dead ahead were combining with the wake of the warship from my port side, making mountainous waves in all directions – a classical, confused sea. By the time I had sorted that lot out, the next ship was passing. I zig-zagged left and right to avoid catching the rollers side-on but was half-way up one wave when it began to break. Frantically I struck out with my paddle, a recovery stroke, then hard left, now hard right trying to pick the most favourable spots. The third ship passed, still in perfect alignment, and I wondered how much more I could take. Stick it out; stick it out! A few more near back-flips and they were passed. I now made an angular course towards Almeirim, one of the last major towns on the Amazon.

There was a small store on the water front from which I bought two kilos of oats, some tinned food and biscuits. They did not have sugar, rice or eggs and I was told I would have to go in to town for them. However, I did not feel like wandering that far from the kayak. Outside the store, a young Negro was cycling around on his pushbike, so I gave him some money and asked if he would nip up to the town and get the provisions for me. This he did and I took a well-earned soft drink while I waited. About ten minutes later he was back, balancing everything on the handlebars. He could have taken off with the money and I would never have found him, so I gave him a good tip to show that honesty pays. His face lit up and so did mine.

I decided some photos would be appropriate and called all the kids down to the kayak. A couple of group snaps and I was on my way.

Finding a camp was not going to be easy in this area because the banks consisted of tidal mangrove swamps, soft mud when the tide was out and inpenetrable mangrove thickets when the tide was in. Just as I was thinking beaches were as scarce as hens' teeth, I struck lucky, a small uncharted sandy island. It was perfect, an ideal spot for cargo reshuffling.

Today is the hundredth day of the trip and an appropriate time for another assessment. Physically, I feel as good as when I started and there is no reason why I should not finish. Ol' kayak has proved very well, considering it was never designed for these conditions. That shooting incident is the only major bad moment so far. Without a doubt it took something from the trip.

Since I am now approaching the final stages, I've made a

more detailed analysis of food supplies and usage. I have got one kilo of milk powder, two kilos of sugar, two kilos of rice, four kilos of oats, two tins of sausages, two tins of sardines, and six eggs. A kilo of oats now lasts less than six days. I estimate I have twenty-one days' supply. A kilo of milk powder lasts fourteen days; a kilo of sugar seven days; a kilo of rice, six days. Also I have eighteen packs of freeze-dried food.

After reloading the stores, I studied the maps. Just beyond here, the river forks into two major channels. About forty miles could be saved by taking the southern channel via Gurupá, but it is quite narrow, less than a mile in parts, and I couldn't be sure I wouldn't run into another trigger-happy idiot. In the northern channel I would be much harder to spot and that made it the logical choice. At Macapá, I could get the last of my major supplies and then island-hop my way back to the southern channel. If I kept going at the present rate, I should reach Cabo Maguari by the end of November and, if ocean conditions were favourable, I should be able to get down the coast to Belém a few days later. From there it was just a plane-ride to London to see my family. My original plan of returning to Lima no longer seemed logical.

Finding a camp site each night got no easier, but the jungle looked beautiful at night, green fireflies flitting around like miniature lanterns and gaps in the canopy where stars shone through. On 22nd November I approached Porto Santana amongst lots of small motor and sail boats, too busy with their own business to be interested in mine. The port was full of foreign-going cargo vessels and the town itself, at the top of a gravel beach, had an excellent range of supplies, oats, milk powder, tinned food, fruit, eggs, sugar, rice, biscuits and batteries. I got the store owner to witness my being there and a large crowd came down to see me off. It was only about nine miles to Macapá but I doubted I would get there before dark. I was not particularly bothered; getting enough supplies to finish the trip was very satisfying. And I could feel Cabo Maguari within my grasp.

A little further downstream from the town, I passed a British ship, the *Benedict*, out of Liverpool. She was tied up in port and I called up to the crew to find me an officer to witness my being there. This they did and Mr Ian Clark, the radio officer, wrote me a note. I laughed when I received the note, as it was so typically British:

Dear Sir,
To Whom it May Concern.
I am the radio officer of MV *Benedict*. During our stay at the port of Santana, Brazil, I was approached by an Australian canoeist, Mr Alan Holman. He asked me to witness his arrival here. It is my pleasure to do so. The date and time is approximately 22 November 1982, 1930 GMT.
Yours sincerely,
Ian M. Clark – Radio Officer.

So, with about one hour of daylight left, it was camp-spot hunting again. The scenery had changed once more. It was back to sandy beaches again and looked rather pleasant. The only problem was that there were houses at every likely camping spot. By 1700 darkness was closing, so I decided to ask permission to camp on a beach near one of the dwellings. After the initial shock of meeting me, the man of the house said no problems, and I was delighted. The family came down to look at ol' kayak and was soon convinced that I was genuinely on an expedition. I thanked them and gave them a tin of corned beef.

It was an excellent beach, soft white sand with coconut palms and a reasonable supply of driftwood. Supper was corned beef, rice pudding and oranges. Then for an hour I watched the stars on a crystal-clear night. A gentle lapping of water on the beach, a tall palm waved gently in the breeze, shooting stars left their trails across the sky. This was my world.

Only sixteen nautical miles up today but that was not important. I had enough supplies to last the rest of the trip and would be home by Christmas.

15   OUT INTO THE OCEAN

On 23rd November I was up at 0400 and got the fire going. I was only eight miles from Macapá and after posting my letters, I would be on the final and possibly most dangerous leg of the trip.

Three plates of porridge, two eggs, an orange and tea for breakfast this morning. Three of the family, the mother and her teenage son and daughter, came down to see how I was getting along. The daughter handed me a piece of sugar cane to eat. The mother was most amused to see me camped against an old tree-trunk. She got a long stick and lifted out a snakeskin to show me. So much for my tropical paradise! Being a residential area, I had neglected my usual check for snakes before sleeping against the trunk.

After exchanging addresses and taking some photographs of the family, I was on my way by 0900. Moderate winds but I stayed in the lee of the bank, where conditions were more favourable. It is commercially a very active region and, once again, I just blended in with the other small ships running to Macapá.

I was there at midday but did not recognise the town at all, it had changed so dramatically in three years. Massive re-development programmes, new buildings, a sealed highway; it is turning into a modern city.

There is a long, tapered beach here which entailed a half-mile walk before reaching the town. A quick jog up the main street (I had no choice – the tarmac was burning my feet), and I got letters to my brother and the Explorers' Club posted. The girl who took them did not know what to make of me, as usual. I still had my buoyancy vest on and was dripping wet. I jogged back to the kayak, feeling very happy. I had a world record now. Nobody else had ever canoed this far down the Amazon and all I had to do was to extend it.

I bought a small rock melon for lunch and sat on the beach checking the charts. It would be about a forty-mile crossing to

174

the southern channel but there were islands in between which I could use as stop-offs. My chart, corrected up to 1979, showed a large bank forming just north of Ilha do Cara, about eight miles from Macapá. If it followed the pattern of most other banks, it would now be pretty close to a permanent island. If it was not, I would just head south for Ilha do Cara itself.

By mid-afternoon I was there and an island had indeed formed about half a mile in diameter with firm tree growth at its peak and low scrub over the rest. I asked the skipper of a large fishing boat the name of the island. "No name," he said, so I guess it had not been officially listed yet. Two of his crew were ashore with shotguns looking for birds and further down the bank was a second interested party. I got the impression they were here with a view to settlement. They watched me carefully as I paddled past and one member of the family followed me round till scrub prevented his further movement. I carried on to the extreme south side of the island where I would be out of sight and hopefully, out of mind.

It was not the best part of the island but at least nobody was laying a claim to it. It was muddy and damp and gave the impression of a snakes' paradise. Dry wood was scarce and I gashed my hand trying to pry dead branches from prickly scrub bushes. My well-earned supper was corned beef, rice pudding, orange, biscuits and chocolate milk.

I was up at 0500 on 24th November and got the breakfast fixed. Since I would be slightly side-on to the rollers for much of the crossing, (my course was approximately south-east), I removed the fin from the kayak. It was very hard to keep a course with waves hitting that and spinning me round.

I was off at 0740. The weather stayed fine but the water was rough. I had to crab my way along, keeping the nose of the kayak into the rollers with a slight bias in the intended direction of travel. It is a very remote area and only an occasional hut could be spotted on some of the islands which are covered in dense low jungle. By 1400, winds intensified and by 1500, I had had enough. Progress was not worth mentioning now.

Two days later I reached the small town of Chaves on the north coast of Marajo. Marajo is a large island, about the size of Switzerland, located in the mouth of the Amazon. The only way to get into the beach was to surf in, although I had no special desire to do so. My poor heavy ol' kayak surfed like a submarine. Its nose stayed under the water and it required a lot of force to manoeuvre it.

I managed to get six eggs and some corned beef and then had the store owner witness me being there. I get the strangest looks. But I'm now used to these and to the crowd who followed me down to the beach to see what I was up to. There were the usual inferences that the kayak was more like a submarine. I hated to admit it, but under the ocean conditions, they were almost right.

I ploughed back out through the surf and made another couple of miles before dark. I had got twenty-four nautical miles up today and my destination was getting closer now.

Winds and light showers kept up for most of the night and made sleep difficult. Being almost on the same longitude as Belém and not more than seventy miles from it, made me wonder if similar weather could be expected here. Belém is renowned for showers. It rains on 245 days of the year.

On 28th November I advanced my watch one hour to Belém time. Adverse winds were now a perpetual state of affairs and the cockpit invariably had a few inches of water in it under these conditions. I found a small amount of seepage in both hatches, too, but it was not unexpected considering the battering ol' kayak was getting. Apart from sore heels from being constantly immersed in water, I was still physically A1. The only effect these conditions were having on me was to increase my appetite.

At 0930 on the twenty-ninth I knew I was in trouble. The kayak was spending more time under the water than on it. I had to battle through half a mile of surf and breakers to get anywhere near unbroken water and by then the cockpit was flooded and conditions kept me too busy to pump it out. It was no use going on, so I surfed back to the beach, very disappointed. Only fifty-five miles to the Cape and I was being stopped. It was hard to say if conditions would improve within days or even weeks. It is wide open to the Atlantic here. Winds and rollers have no obstacles in their path.

I spent the morning assessing the stores situation and tried to predict how long I could sit things out waiting for better weather. At present consumption rates, I estimated I could last for nine days.

Next day I gave it another try, bulldozing through the surf. I was half a mile out and the spray cover got torn loose and the cockpit flooded. It was one hell of a battle to hold the kayak into the waves and pump at the same time. I resecured the spray cover, but waves were pounding over me and tearing it loose again. The kayak was hardly ever above the water. It was no good. I had to go back in.

Morale was really low now. So close to the Cape but I could not reach it. The kayak was just too heavy for these surfy, foamy waters. They would not support its weight. Something I had not taken into consideration until now was the weight of the kayak itself. After almost four months in the river the fibreglass must have absorbed a fair amount of water. How many extra kilos I did not know, but it could be significant.

I sat on the beach dismally nibbling biscuits and suddenly the penny dropped. What were those two beautiful, inflatable compensators for along the side of the kayak? They would help it ride higher in the water. Why I had overlooked them, I do not know.

A quick inflation, a check for leaks, and it was back into action. Now the kayak was riding higher and looked a lot less like a submarine. Very few waves were breaking over the cockpit. Drag was predictably increased, but we were going somewhere. I just kept slogging along all day – we're going to make it, ol' kayak!

By 1800 I pulled in to a bank near Vila Nazare. Thirteen nautical miles up today and that beat sitting on a sandbank.

By 1100 next morning I was travelling at a staggering two knots! Winds and chops were definitely down today and the going was easier. A large trawler pulled alongside thinking I might be in trouble. I gave the thumbs-up I'm OK sign and they carried on. An hour later, another one did the same, but they appeared really baffled. The captain pointed to the sky and wanted to know if I was a survivor from an aircraft. I guessed the bright orange compensators gave the appearance of a life-raft. No, I assured him, I am OK and going to Belém.

It is difficult for people who spend their lives battling the elements to eke out a meagre living to comprehend why anybody would be doing it for adventure. The trawler followed for another half-hour until the Ilha Camaleao. The captain was still scratching his head as we parted company.

At 1500 I encountered a sailing boat just pulling out from the mainland. As expected, and in true tradition of the sea, he wanted to know if I was OK. I gave him the thumbs-up sign and he was off. We were both heading in the same direction, easterly and into the wind. The sailboat was fairly sleek and fast but it was unable to get close to the wind. He was making some very impressive tacks of about two miles on each leg, battling his way up the coast, but was unable to get any distance in front of me as I plodded along in a straighter line at probably less than two knots. After the sixth leg, he realised his predicament, lowered the sail and the whole family took to the oars.

The type of sail he was using gave the appearance of a harp and probably dated back to the times of the early settlers. It was grossly inefficient and I doubted if he could get closer than within seventy degrees of the eye of the wind. A few simple modifications to sail and boat could have vastly improved his lot.

By 1700, tides had turned and winds intensified and I was in irons, as the old sailors would say. There was no shortage of sandy beaches, parts of the North Marajo coastline would consist of miles of unbroken sand dunes, while other places would resemble a tropical paradise with palm trees waving in the breeze and a soft gentle beach below. Still others would be typical dense Amazon jungles. My only worry was how high the tide could reach tonight; it was a full moon. I set up camp at the highest point on the beach, just at the edge of the jungle. I got fifteen nautical miles up today and, according to my charts, I was forty-eight degrees fifty minutes west of Greenwich. Diagonally across from me I could see the signal lamp on Ilha do Machadinho flashing. The next signal lamp would be the Cape and my mind was locked to it like a radar scanner on to its target.

The water was still fresh, although it was getting more murky by the day. I usually gathered water from the pools on the beach as these would have had time to settle out. I still practised my survival drills, just in case the need should arise. If no fresh water was available here, what would I do? There was an abundance of tall coconut palms in the area but climbing them might not be wise. However, the trunks were not so very thick so I could always saw or even burn through them, to bring the coconuts down. There would be no need to die of thirst or starvation here.

Friday, 3rd December I was awakened by some wild boars snorting around the camp. They did not seem to be any threat but I would rather they were not here. A couple of heavy logs thrown in their direction sent them packing.

The weather was fair but it had been blowing all night and everything was covered in sand. The water was unbelievably murky and looked like thick gravy.

A couple of men visited the camp whilst I was having breakfast. They were carrying a rifle and were hunting boars. They asked me if I had seen any, so I showed them the tracks and they followed on.

I was too impatient to wait for high tide and bulldozed my way out through the surf at 0945. My impatience did not pay off. I got a mile or so out from the beach and stopped there. Winds and currents held me firm. I did not like going back in so I just sat out there marking time. It was ninety minutes before the tide turned and I felt an idiot for wasting that much time.

By 1130 I was definitely moving east and I was excited as hell. The wind and chop abated slightly and I kept digging that paddle in. A couple of trawlers turned off course to see if I was OK and I gave the usual thumbs-up and they passed on. I felt a little guilty when they had to deviate from course for me, but such is the age-old tradition of the sea.

By 1430 I was rounding the Cape. Banco São Rogue, a large sandbank at the Cape, is now an established island with a small hut on it and two fishing boats tied up along side. My three-year-old chart had it as a sub-service sandbank.

A sudden change in water colour came to my attention and I took a handful to taste. Yes, it was salty! I had a litre of fresh water on board and that would do for tonight.

I rounded the island and at 1600 pulled up beneath the Cape Maguari signal lamp. I thank my God, I am sure He was close at times. I am so happy that I hug ol' kayak. Good ol' kayak! Good ol' kayak – we made it!

Saturday, 4th December I was up at 0430, my fire still smouldering so I had just to stoke it up a bit. I made two plates of porridge with salt water. They were palatable but not the best.

Two fishermen passed along the beach and I asked for information on fresh water. They pointed to a couple of houses half a mile inland and told me I could get water there. I grabbed all the containers I could find and followed them along a rough track through farmland.

There were two family groups living here, ten people in all and they appeared quite well off by local standards, with chickens, pigs and a cow, good quality houses, a couple of motorised fishing vessels in a nearby creek and a few farm animals. They certainly did not want for anything.

After filling the containers, I was given a cup of Brazilian coffee and we had a discussion about my trip. Everybody seemed interested and I was invited to stay for lunch. By now, everybody wanted to see ol' kayak and so we all returned to the beach.

After I'd showed them how I lived, one of the ladies offered to polish my badly burned billy can for me. I declined the offer saying I would only need it for a few more days. I had noticed throughout the trip the pride both Indians and mestizos took in cleaning cooking pots.

To round the morning off, I got my camera out and took some group photos and movies, then back to the house for lunch.

One of the men cut me down eight coconuts and with a razor-sharp machete skilfully removed all the surplus covering from them so that I could fit them into the kayak.

Fish and rice for lunch, plus a little corned beef from the tin I had donated. This was followed by another cup of Brazilian coffee and by then I felt so comfortable I almost cancelled the day's canoeing!

We exchanged addresses, I put my name in the family book and promised to send the photographs on. No money would be accepted for the food or coconuts so I used the only alternative method and made a 500-cruzeiro gift for the children.

Winds would no longer be adverse for this part of the trip. I was now heading south to south-west. The only possible problem was being side-on to the Atlantic rollers. I might have to crab my way down the coast.

The kayak was really heavy with eight litres of water and eight coconuts for extra cargo. The swell was down and out I went. There was a massive sandbank to get round, Banco Rabo da Onca. I have to go three miles out before turning south. Currents and winds were favourable, but I was seldom pointing in the intended direction of travel.

The bank extends seven miles to the south and I reached Ponta Fina by 1715, only six nautical miles in the required direction, but I have travelled at least ten. It is sixty nautical miles to Belém and so long as I could find water, I would be OK.

The tide was out and the closest I could get to shore was within half a mile, so I beached the kayak and inspected the area. There were a couple of coral-clustered tree stumps and a large rip channel that would not have been very nice to step into on a turning tide in pitch darkness. I returned to the kayak and ate a coconut whilst waiting for the tide.

At 1830 it turned and for the next two and a half hours I walked the kayak in, foot by foot. I just held the deck line and let the sea carry it in a little at a time. It was something like taking a dog for a walk, that wanted to stop every few paces. It needed a lot of patience. There was no moon up and care was needed as the tide moved in around me.

At 2100 I was high and dry on the sand dunes and got camp organised. The wind was blowing strongly now and I had to start the fire in a plastic bag. After chocolate rice pudding made with fresh water, I rested contentedly on the beach. Nobody lived near here, just miles of sand dunes and nothing to support habitation.

Only another week or so and I would be in England. But I would miss this lifestyle. It was costing me almost nothing to live, I enjoyed the camps, and even my crude cooking. What had the rat race to offer me? Hotel and restaurant bills, lots of traffic noise and pollution. I would need a lot more clothes, especially in Europe, and of course a pair of shoes to imprison my feet once more. And then, back to work for two to three years until I had enough money for another adventure. What was the rush?

At 2300 I crawled into the sack and listened to the winds and surf. It is a beautiful world.

The fire was still smouldering next morning as I had covered it with sand. There was no rush to be off as the tide would not be in for hours. Beef casserole, two plates of porridge and a coconut for breakfast. Winds were blowing strongly, the surf was high and I was not really happy about it. At 1015 I took off and forced my way out. About half a mile from the beach, a large breaker back-flipped the kayak and ejected me from the cockpit. More by luck than judgement I was holding the deck line. One of the compensators had been ripped off, the fin shattered and I was worried. Getting back into the kayak proved impossible. It was flooded and like a great dead log rolling over and over. I got exhausted and committed the cardinal sin of letting the paddle go. Conditions were foul in all directions and I had no idea which way the current flowed. I seemed to be drifting south, but whether I was moving in to the beach or away was hard to say. I made a few promises that I hope one day to keep, and eventually found myself surging back through the surf and foam, over and over we rolled until finally we were in.

Poor ol' kayak had taken a battering and I decided it was time to call it a day and put her to rest. I had got my longed-for world record so why push my luck in trying to do something the kayak was not designed for?

Souré is only twenty-five miles down the coast and I could walk there in a couple of days. It is a large town and I would be able to get a ship to Belém from there easily.

My map and paddle were washed up further down the beach but it looked like King Neptune had claimed my hat. I feel lucky to have got in – things need not have worked out that way.

I spent the day unloading the kayak and packing what I needed into a holdall. My binoculars, cameras, clothes, food and water. I even made a RIP (Rest In Peace) sign for ol' kayak.

She's going to spend the rest of her days atop the sand dunes looking out to sea.

Before supper, I tried carrying the holdall along the beach on my back. It was bulky and most uncomfortable. A rucksack would be fine, but an awkward bag digging into my back under the tropical sun would not be tolerable for long. It was time for a big re-think.

I re-checked my maps of the area and realised I had been too hasty. Following the coastline around was considerably more than twenty-five miles. Also, there were some fairly large creeks I would have to cross and where was the next supply of fresh water? I hate going back on a decision, but ol' kayak might be the only way. I spent the evening thinking over the possibilities. Just after midnight, I got up to observe the tide. It was on its way out and not looking dangerous. Perhaps I would be lucky tomorrow.

Monday, 6th December I was up at 0600 and started repairs on the kayak. The fin was beyond repair and unsuited to the conditions anyway, so I dumped it. I relashed the compensators using shock cord and heavy-duty tie wraps. I made a chin strap for my spare hat and fitted the second blade on to the spare paddle, which then became too long to carry on the bow so I secured it along the stern, behind me. A single-bladed emergency paddle is not much use under these conditions.

At 1100 I had breakfast and lunch combined. Two plates of porridge with fifty per cent salt water and fifty per cent fresh and a tin of corned beef.

At 1300 I was off and before I got 100 yards out, I got back-flipped again and returned to the beach. I waited another ninety minutes and tried once more. The surf was much lower now and I made it this time. I was a mile out and apart from the odd breaker that gave me a series of mini heart attacks, progress was fair. As the tide attenuated, conditions improved and I was making miles. By 1800 I was at Ponta de Galos and that was eight miles up for the day.

On 7th December, a horseman woke me up. He was a farm worker making his way up the coast. I asked how long it took by horse from Souré. Three hours, he said, but it could only be done when the tide was out. Well, at least now I knew it could be done on foot.

At 1230 it was time to go but the surf was too high. I decided to try dragging my kayak through the shallows by its deck line until conditions improved. It worked OK, except the kayak kept running into the back of my legs or up on to the beach. I stayed knee-deep in water and kept plodding on. The cockpit had to be pumped out every fifteen minutes or so but I was making ground. I canoed across the bays and more sheltered areas and this gave my legs a rest.

At 1330 I spotted a small farm house along the beach and tried for water. A Negro family lived here and if the eyes are the window of the soul, then I had come to the wrong house. A couple of the men looked really mean. However, the mother and daughter seemed indifferent and ladled me a litre of water from their jug. I carried on dragging the kayak down the beach and soon a couple of men followed me. They were not armed, so I was not bothered. They started asking for money but I told them I did not have any. The youngest one made a sexual gesture which I ignored. They followed for about a quarter of a mile and then turned back. Small instances like that tended to spoil the day.

The surf remained high for most of the afternoon, so it's half walking, half canoeing. But by evening I had made seven nautical miles and conditions were much the same the next day when a few more huts and a lot more shipping told me I was close to Souré.

By 1500 I was at the harbour entrance and made my last camp. I got all my washing done and fixed a supper of coconut, sliced lamb and peas, followed by a chocolate-flavoured rice pudding. At 2030 I was in to bed and have seldom felt more contented in my life.

Next day I found a cargo boat, the *Iate Formigosa*, which would take me and ol' kayak to Belém. We departed at 2300 along with a cargo of fruit and a pig. The fare was 500 cruzeiros ($1.50 US) and for that you slept on the deck. Once clear of the harbour, the tri-sail was raised and remained filled for the duration of the trip.

By 0600 we were heading into Belém harbour and I spotted *Calypso* again. She was sailing for Martinique within the hour. I went aboard for a coffee and Mme Cousteau gave me yet another Cousteau Society T-shirt. Most of the crew were disembarking for Christmas leave and they helped me to pull the kayak up on to the wharf. I threw away all my well-worn T-shirts and my sleeping-sack.

I am unbelievably happy. Things have worked out extremely well. I have had a lot of good luck, met a lot of wonderful people, and have achieved a longed-for ambition.

After checking into a hotel and getting cleaned up, I try to readjust to the world. I feel fine. I feel wonderful, just light on my feet and hungry. Walking on paved streets is a strange experience for me and remained so for almost a week.

I have lost around five kilos on the trip and surprised myself at how much I could eat in this first week. I could get through a three-course lunch and within less than an hour be hungry again. I would buy a king-sized hamburger, or perhaps some icecream, and within an hour of that I would need something else. It was fortunate that Belém was so cheap, or I would have been bankrupt. At first I worried that I might have some Amazonian creature living inside me, but gradually my craving for food lessened.

On 16th December we had a small handing-over ceremony when I donated ol' kayak to the Rowers' Club of Belém as a memento of my trip, and on 20th December I left Brazil for England.

I had canoed approximately 3800 miles in 116 days, descending from about 3000 feet at Quiteni in the Andes, 230 miles from the Pacific Ocean, to the Atlantic at Cape Maguari, entirely on my own, propelled by my own muscle power and financed entirely by my own efforts. I had made the *Guinness Book of Records* as the person who had canoed the greatest distance down the Amazon. Moreover, I had accomplished this without any calamities either to myself or to good ol' kayak. As Chris Bonington once wrote of adventurers, audacity has a momentum that carries its own protection.

As a final note, I would like to say that for all the condemnation of South America's political systems, I was allowed to go wherever I wanted, talk to whoever I pleased, and even stay wherever I liked. I met from the richest to the poorest and moved among them without restriction. Any country that allows that doesn't have too much to hide.

Appendix I Cargo List

Medical Kit
Sunglasses	
Waterproof plasters	12
Eucalyptus oil	0.1 litre
Water puritabs	400
Tweezers	
Antiseptic cream	1 tube
Blockout cream	2 tubes
Maloprin	50
Aspirin	50
Achrostatin	150
Lomotil	100
Salt tablets	100
Multivitamins	200
Cotton wool	

Repair Kit
Waterproof tape	4 rolls
Nylon rope	30m
Small saw	
Hacksaw blades	4
Small file	
Shock cord	15m
Fibreglass roller	
Fibreglass resin	1.5kg
Fibreglass mat	2m^2
Fibreglass cloth	5m^2
Measuring cups	4
Abrasive paper	10 sheets
Paint brushes	4
Acetone	0.5 litre
Plastic glue	2 tubes
Silicone rubber	1 tube
Tie wraps	50
Pump diaphragms	2
Pump 'O' ring kit	
Plastic tubing 1½"	0.3m
Misc screws and fittings	

Food
Freeze-dried food	40 packs
Oats	0.5kg
Milk powder	0.5kg
Sugar	0.3kg
Tea bags	20
Coffee	50gm
Saccharin tablets	200

Money
160,000 soles
$1100 US Travellers' cheques
$800 US cash

Personal Hygiene
Shaving razor	
Soap	1 bar
½ towel	
Dentist mirror	
Toothpaste	1 tube
Toothbrush	
Hairbrush	
Comb	
Body talc	100gm
Toilet paper	1 roll

Clothes Container
Shorts	1 pair
Socks	2 pairs
Sport shirt	1
Polo neck	2
Pants	2
Hats	2
T-shirts	1
Spray jacket	1
Plastic poncho	1
Vaccination cert.	
Photostat copies – letters of introduction	

CARGO LIST

Items Worn
Buoyancy vest
Sport shirt
Gym shoes
Socks
Wrist bands
Shorts
Pants
Sunglasses
Watch

Cameras
Movie camera
Movie films — 10
Still camera
Still films — 3
Lens brush
Spare batteries — 4
Flash gun
Timer

Camping Gear
Canopy kit
Space blanket
Mosquito net
Camper mat
Hammock
Gas lighter
Matches – waterproof — 6 boxes
Flashlamp
Billy can (0.5 litre cap)
Frying-pan
Aluminium plate
Fork, spoon, plastic cup

Misc
Spare watch
Solar panel
Batteries (rechargeable) — 4
Bulbs — 4
Pen

Pencil
Notebook
Envelopes — 4
Tape measure
Hooks — 100
Fishing line — 200m
Plastic egg box
Cotton — 2 reels
Needles — 6
Buttons — 6
Clothes pegs — 6
Carborundum stone
Dictionaries (Span & Port) — 2
Log (diary)
Thongs (flip-flops) — 1 pair
Nylon holdalls — 2
Mini rucksack
Air pillows — 2
Reflectors — 10
Reflective tape
AUS stickers — 2
Elastic bands — 30
Plastic jug (1 litre)
Sponge
Washing powder — 0.25kg
Wave deflector
Fin
Sheath knives — 2
Pocket knife
Charts/maps — 1.8kg
Paddle blades — 4
Aluminium shafts — 2
White-water paddle
Touring paddle
Compasses — 3
Dividers — 1 pair
Binoculars — 1 pair
Parallel rulers — 1
Sealable plastic bags — 15
Spring-balance

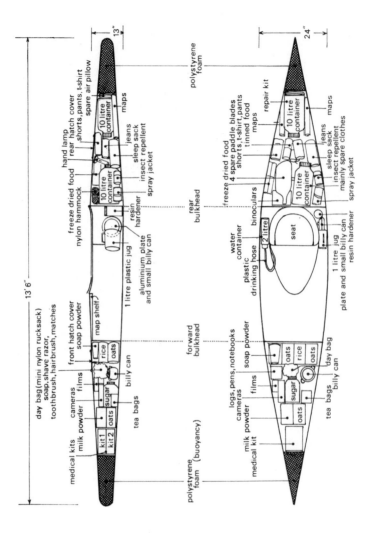

Basic Cargo Configuration

Appendix II   Glossary Of Terms

Boil:	Boiling action of water (appearance of). Caused by obstructions on the river bed.
Confused water:	Water that has no direction – unpredictable.
Eddy:	A contrary current flow, often found on the inside of bends or behind obstructions protruding above the surface of the river.
Ferry glide:	Method of traversing a river by keeping the nose of the craft into the flow, with a slight bias in direction of intended travel. Used where conditions are too dangerous to allow a craft to be side-on to the flow.
Freeze-dried foods:	Basically a modern method of dehydrating foods that doesn't damage the cell structure and retains all the goodness.
Mestizo:	Person of mixed race, e.g. Spanish/Indian.
One-man rescue:	As the name implies, to be able to rescue oneself without assistance.
Paddle park:	Clamp for holding paddle.
Portage:	To carry a canoe, e.g. around a rapid.
River and Rapid grades:	Rivers are graded by canoeists into a numbered system from one to six depending on the degree of difficulty, severity of conditions and the likely consequences of making a mistake. However, rapids or individual sections of a river may vary considerably in grades. Grade one to two would have small rapids and drops and simple obstructions, whereas a grade six is a definite threat to life with long and violent rapids, whirlpools and steep gradients.
Space blanket:	A development of the space age. A thin plastic blanket one side of which has a reflective surface. Heat can be reflected away from or in towards a person depending which direction the reflective surface is facing.

189

Spray cover: Also called 'spray deck' or 'roll cover'. A cover that prevents water from entering the cockpit area. It is secured around the waist of the canoeist and over the cockpit combing.

Stopper: Standing wave caused by fast-flowing shallow water running into a deeper and slower-moving section of the river.

Whirl: Whirlpool-type action. A vortex of water.

White water: Such as found in mountainous areas, fast flowing and giving a foaming boiling action as it passes restrictions and obstructions.

Windage: The area of a vessel that wind can act on (i.e. all above the water line).

Yawing: A snake-like movement, zig-zagging.